Winning Strategies for Women

Bethany Williams

Preface:

I wrote the first edition of *Winning Strategies* when GE was acquiring the company that I worked for: IDX Systems Corporation. It was a stressful, difficult time and many feared for their jobs and their futures. I wanted to give women the confidence to venture out and achieve the success, positions, and financial pay that they were striving to attain. Often they were sluggish to move, apprehensive, and they were letting fear drive their paths.

I'm excited that since publication, the book has travelled continents, and encouraged and blessed women in India, the United Kingdom, Singapore, China, Canada, and the United States.

Emails come in from around the globe and I'm continually humbled that an effort to help others within my small circle to achieve has resulted in such splendid international outcomes.

My wish for you is to find a nugget in this book that solidifies your resolve to go further, press ahead, and achieve the goals and aspirations that you have set for yourself. I hope that you find—as I did in my life—that they are all worth chasing and certainly many of them will be fruitful.

Best wishes and good luck in your journey. You *can* help yourself to keep your job. You can make more money and receive the choice assignments and the positions that you want. **Regardless of gender, companies cannot ignore obvious success.** Once you recognize a few basic aides and killers that can either catapult or hamper your trip up the ladder, success is not far away. In 12 chapters, we will review the keys to success. Walk through this mentoring advice with an eye on how it can affect you, your work life, and your future. It is intended to be a quick and easy read. Read on for further information on "your trip up the ladder."

Author's Note: The editor has revised this edition to include "Advice in Action," containing snippets of emails, tweets, conversations or comments from my blog [http://bethanywilliams.info]. These women either have read the first edition, heard me speak, or I've mentored them personally. We've abbreviated their names to protect their employment status – grin. We hope you will take action to advance your career, find your strengths, and raise your pay too!

Winning Strategies for Women **Advice in Action**
"Bethany,
You have the ability to turn on lights for many that are dark about their lives and careers. You wake up those that are sleeping at their desks in jobs that don't bring them joy and remind us that playing it safe does not always get us ahead. Thank you for reminding us to continue to make a difference for our companies, in our lives, and the lives of our fellow employees." Lynn F., Dallas, Texas

"Hello Bethany,
My name is K. W. and I just wanted to say hello. You are very encouraging and inspiring. I checked your website out and found it to be very informative. I will definitely go out and purchase your book. Thank you and I wish you continued success in all that you do." S. W., Singapore

Winning Strategies for Women

New Edition

Mentoring Advice to Help You Advance at Work

Bethany Williams

Winning Strategies Book 1

ISBN-13:
978-1466361881

ISBN-10:
1466361883

Second edition: March 2012

For more information or to contact the author visit:
http://www.BethanyAWilliams.com

Printed in the United States of America

Table of Contents

Chapter One

1. Confidence: How Do You Get It?

Fake it 'til you Make it!

I discovered the glamorous world of fashion and modeling as a teenager. The New York scene was awe-inspiring. Models from all over the world convene on New York City to attempt to obtain agent representation. There are only a few agents and seas of models. Models are sent on 'go-sees' that send them from one agent to another, trying to get an agent to believe that they are the next Tyra Banks.

The models arrive in a large room filled with tables laden with agents, lined up row after row. Picture hundreds of beautiful, skinny, well-groomed lovelies all rushing for the chance for representation. The pit of your stomach tells you to run quickly out the door to the first bus stop to purchase tickets to your hometown. Every bit of your confidence is waning. Your mind is pointing out every fault that you have, one that the girl next to you surely doesn't have. You meet the first agent with another model from your agency. The agent says to her, "Why would I use you, you have a scar on your forehead. There are thousands of girls with no scar, get a clue!" Your stomach drops as you wonder what he will say to you. You walk with her over to the next table where the next agent says to her, "You have exactly the look that I've been searching for." She walks away with a contract and representation, only seconds after a horrendous put down from the first agent.

In this bazaar world, you learn something very important. You quickly discover that one person's opinion is just that: one opinion. You learn that it can be completely opposite from the opinion of the next person you encounter. Early on, you begin lifting your head up high, walking and speaking with the confidence of a model who has been at it for many years. You quickly learn to "fake it 'till you make it," feigning confidence until you can build it within. That unfounded confidence and bold belief in yourself will make others believe in you too.

Key Point: Don't Let Your Confidence Be Easily Swayed.

One person's opinion is just that: ONE opinion. It may prove to be completely opposite of the next opinion you receive.

This scenario can be seen in action in your business life. Many employees sit back and watch "green" employees take on an assignment that is going to be difficult for them. You were at the same table. You heard the assignment offered. You believed that you would do a great job. You lacked a bit of confidence in yourself. You didn't volunteer for the promotion or the assignment. You would have been great at it.

You need to believe in yourself. If you don't believe in yourself, how can you expect others to? Let's face it: you know yourself. Think through several positions for which you didn't apply. Mentally shuffle through several chances you had to introduce yourself to top-level executives. Review in your mind the opportunities that you didn't take because you were shy, insecure, or lacked confidence. Prepare a written description of how you would respond if given those chances again. For example, prepare an example for how you might introduce yourself to the most senior executive/General Manager/CEO at your organization:

Hello, Mr./Ms _____, I don't think we've met. My name is Emily Miller, I work in the _____ Division on the _____ project. It's nice to finally meet you.

Concentrate on a very basic introduction. Practice this until it flows off your tongue easily and with confidence. In this 'fake it till you make it' world, you are an equal to this senior executive. Your ideas are equally as important, just like your time. However, the introduction isn't the right place to pitch your latest idea. After all, you didn't intend to run into him/her. It's enough to recognize higher-level executives with confidence, and give them an opportunity to get to know you.

This thought makes a lot of us nervous. We are afraid of saying the wrong thing, or coming off in a negative light. Think of yourself as a product. The advertising and messaging around the product make it look good. The messages are carefully crafted and the target audiences are identified before the message has gone out. Keep this in mind. This will be discussed more in a future chapter on Touting Your Success. At this point in the book, concern yourself only with confidence building and the ability to fake confidence every step of the way.

Key Point: Think of Yourself as a Product.

This product—YOU—is packaged, branded, and advertised just like any other product or service that you buy or sell. Construct your "message" carefully.

Feigning confidence doesn't preclude you from asking numerous questions or getting input from across the organization. Actually, both steps are very necessary in moving your ideas forward, and pushing the company to excel at what they do.

Trusting in Yourself

Mentoring women often allows me to see the big picture. In mentoring and interviewing women to fill open positions, I have noticed a theme worthy of elaboration. Women often say that they're not right for the job. Many say they have been home raising children for several years and aren't sure if they would be any good, or what position they could fill. It is important to trust in your skills and abilities. We want to paint an accurate picture, one that involves hard work no matter the setting. But we tend to point out our weaknesses—not our strengths—without even realizing it. Our male counterparts, on the other hand, tend to point out their strengths, not their weaknesses. This makes filling the position easy for the hiring manager. Whom would you hire? Someone who says, "I have been

4

home raising children for the last few years, but I can probably do the job." Or, the one who says, "I am the right person for the job. I have skills that will benefit the company and I am capable and willing to get the job done." It's not even a competition. We need CONFIDENCE. We need to check our misgivings at the door. This is a great time to act MORE confident than you feel. It is a great time to trust in your abilities and to speak with confidence. You are your advertising agent, press agent, public relations staff, negotiations manager, and confidante. If you don't believe in yourself, neither will others. What do you have to lose? Go for it!

Winning Strategies Advice in Action: Strengths and Successes

"I don't know how to sell my skills and qualifications as a consultant.
I was at the meeting on Monday and heard you speak. I thought you were terrific.
For the last 16 years, I had a successful career in Human Resources. Three years ago, I decided to stay home with my kids (I traveled so much that it was causing stress in the family). I opened a consulting firm but it has not had the success that I wanted. I have always considered myself to be a very confident person in everything I do. Recently, I know I don't have any direction, which is greatly affecting my confidence level. Are you able to offer any advice or suggestions? Sincerely," Nancy H., New Jersey

"We as women often struggle with selling ourselves. We see our weaknesses, and in our eyes, they are often bigger than our strengths. Think about your

successful career. What made it successful? Highlight those strengths and repeat those in your mind. Add quantifiable benefits to those strengths. Were you able to save X dollars, or facilitate a $x dollar project? Look at your experience through the eyes of an owner. Document your strengths and focus there, in both online media (like LinkedIn) as well as in-person interviews. I know that you will do great. Best Wishes." ~ Bethany

◆ ◆ ◆ ◆ ◆ ◆

Key Point: Trust in Yourself!

Trusting and believing in yourself is vital. Find it within yourself to embrace confidence. When you believe in yourself, others will believe in you too.

◆ ◆ ◆ ◆ ◆ ◆

What *really* gets in our way? We do. We get in our own way. Our lack of self-confidence keeps us from applying for and requesting the positions in which we would succeed.

It takes time to figure this out. You may have figured it out the hard way, as others have. Maybe you have watched positions become available. You watched several people apply. You didn't apply, thinking that you weren't ready or you were just fearful of not getting the position and then having to live with rejection. Your fear and lack of confidence held you back. The new-hire then struggles for the next year or so and eventually quits or gets fired. When is it that you find the confidence to apply for the position?

Did you train the new hires? Did you spend time working with them to orient them to the culture and to the people? Why didn't you apply for the position? The second or third time the position comes open, we then find it within ourselves to 'go for it!'

> ### *Winning Strategies* **Advice in Action: Confidence**
> Bethany helped me to realize that "I can do that!"
> Carla M., Dallas, Texas

So, why don't we believe in ourselves the first time around? Why are we afraid of taking the risk? Nothing is gained without risk. No one faults you for trying to advance, even if you don't succeed. Keep thinking this way. I can guarantee that you will never advance if you don't at least try. Take the first step; it's the hardest. The tricky part is to apply with every confidence that you will get it. Then accept the results with a gracious attitude if you do not get the position.

Having a great mentor will help you through the process; they can give you pointed and honest input when you are hitting a blank wall. I once asked my mentor why she felt that I hadn't gotten a promotion very early in my career. She pointed out that although I was very skilled, I didn't have a college education. (Be prepared not to like what your mentor has to say. Sometimes the answers are not what you are expecting.) For days, I sat around depressed about my situation. A boyfriend said to me, "Well, just go and get your college education." His advice seemed crazy to me: I was a single mom, living on a very small wage, in California of all places. It was one of the most expensive places to live in the nation. Money was already tight; how was I going to pay for a college education? I worked long hours; when was I going to attend school? "Well," he said, "if you would stop feeling sorry for yourself long enough, you could figure out a way to get a college education." That stuck with me. We concentrate on the problems more than we concentrate on finding the solutions. I couldn't afford to stay at my present pay forever. I hadn't done my homework, so I had no knowledge of federal grants, state grants, or financial aid. I had convinced myself that there was no way out of the situation. Kevin believed I could do it all along.

Why do we allow others to have more belief in us than we have in ourselves? I am confident that there is some barrier in your life that you have convinced yourself that you cannot overcome. You believe that it's impossible, even though you haven't done your homework. You haven't researched the possibilities. You really can overcome it.

I enrolled in college at National University, a college for working adults. The instructors at these universities work full-time in the fields that they teach; therefore, your education is immediately applied to the work that you do. A judge taught the Business Law class. A marketing executive that ran his own firm taught the Marketing Class. He handled the marketing campaign for Crest Toothpaste, AND he wrote the marketing book that we used in the class. It was the same book used at the state universities, only we got the author as the instructor. I loved the classes and the chance to pursue my education while working. So, what is holding you back? Day after day, I mentor women to discover what is holding them back and to devise a plan to move them forward. It starts with a simple action plan.

I was able to complete my Bachelors degree in three years. My daughter used to say that when she turned eight years old, mommy would be out of college. We both anxiously had awaited that day.

You can tackle the barriers in your life that are holding you back. How do you motivate yourself to do the homework and the research? How do you take the first step toward knocking down your barrier? Read on to discover ways to motivate yourself to achieve more.

Motivating Yourself

Motivating yourself is an essential ability to develop to advance your career, your pay, and your movement up the corporate ladder. You need to be able to 'get things done' to include some of the tasks and projects that you often shove aside. To succeed, we need to accomplish the important tasks, even the ones that we don't like to do. This ability to recognize the important tasks and be able to get them done will allow you to stand out from the crowd. But, how do you motivate yourself to do things you don't like to do? How do you motivate yourself to do things that seem cumbersome and difficult to accomplish? Read on for your solution.

Motivating yourself is simple. You know yourself better than anyone in the world does. You know your cravings and desires. You will use this knowledge of yourself to dangle carrots in front of the tasks necessary to push you to the next level.

Three years into my career, I decided that I would begin to apply for promotions. I was driving an inexpensive Hyundai and desperately wanted a car with a bit more sizzle. I pinned a picture of a little red convertible on my board at the office. In the car sat a picture of me with my daughter. It became my motivation. I was visualizing what success would look like. If I could pull off the promotion I wanted, I would allow myself to go and buy that Capri convertible in Candy Apple Red. Visualize the success that you want to attain. Think about the reward that you would give yourself if you could achieve that success. I eventually got the promotion—and the convertible. I became the youngest director at the hospital. I was happiest about the car and my hair blowing in the wind.

Not long ago I met with a 19-year old college student named Susan. She was struggling with an inability to quit smoking, although she hadn't been smoking for very long. She feared that it left an impression that she didn't want to leave behind. She was interviewing for jobs. When asked what motivated her, she said shopping. She loved to spend money. She set up a plan to pay herself $10 a day for up to twenty days if she could quit smoking. If successful, she would pay herself in one lump sum on the twentieth day. She would then allow herself to go on a $200 shopping spree for attaining her goal. The first eight days were the hardest for her. Happily, she achieved her goal. This is a tough example. I'm not recommending that you start with such a difficult task. Some are never able to quit smoking; however, Susan was new enough to it that she was able to motivate herself out of the habit.

Lisa, a single mother with three teenage girls, consistently struggled with motivation. There were so many things that she wanted to accomplish; yet, she often felt depressed and unable to focus. Her to-do list was long, and her not-done list was even longer. She was not motivated to accomplish her list. To her, it represented just another thing that she had to do. She started by making the list smaller and attaching rewards to each item on the list. She was able to apply for a promotion at work, sell her house, and began moving her life in the direction she wanted.

Many successful women continue to reward themselves throughout life. I recommend it as a proven method for even the best procrastinators. I speak publicly, regularly, for my job. Even after ten years of public speaking and presentations, I continue to reward myself with chocolate bars for a successful presentation. It still works. You can quickly identify your favorite rewards. If you don't accomplish enough or if you feel that you could have done better, then withhold your reward. You will be amazed at the results.

Key Point: Learn Ways to Motivate Yourself.

Figure out ways to motivate yourself to get things done. Identify rewards that motivate you to accomplish tasks and projects.

Use this reward theory for large assignments at the office as well. There are pieces of administrative duties at your job that you don't like to do, as well as areas that are just plain hard to accomplish. These could be extensive assignments or write ups. If it is an extensive assignment, than consider allowing yourself a new blouse or a new outfit upon completion. The reward should match the effort required to achieve it.

For small assignments, try requiring that you finish it before you get a cup of coffee or go for lunch. Amazingly, you will be able to get through the most monotonous task for a cup of java or the reward of food.

Think of a few things that would motivate you and write them here:

Small Motivators:

_____

_____

_____

_____

Big Motivators:

_____

_____

_____

Now, consider either the things that you don't like to do, or the things you struggle with getting done. What could you motivate yourself to do?

Small tasks you could motivate yourself to do:

_____

Large tasks you could motivate yourself to do:

_____

I'll be interested to hear how successful you are at accomplishing the tasks as you begin to reward yourself.

Try locking yourself in your office and not coming out until you complete the assignment. You may come out looking a little rough, but you will accomplish those laborious tasks.

> ### _Winning Strategies_ **Advice in Action: Motivation**
> "I realize that I can use self-motivation combined with hard work, mentoring and networking to make my place in the sun." Karla F., Boston, Massachusetts

Knowing/Finding Your Strengths

A valuable exercise is to know and understand the strengths that you possess. These strengths assist you when knowing what assignments to volunteer for and what type of positions to apply for. You are uniquely gifted with strengths. You are different from anyone else. These innate strengths power your passions and your abilities. Many women are well into their 30s or 40s before they know what their strengths are. Knowing these early on in your career will be helpful in defining your career growth and path.

What are your strengths? Think about the things that you most like to do. You are energized when you use your strengths. You never tire of doing these tasks; rather, you volunteer for them. They are what you like to do. If you had a job truly utilizing your strengths, you would enjoy it greatly, you would do very well, and you would be very successful at it. Your goal is to understand your strengths *so well* that you strive to move into a position that uses those strengths on a daily basis—if you aren't already.

If you don't know your strengths and are struggling to understand where to start, I recommend Marcus Buckingham's book *Now, Discover Your Strengths*. It includes a 'test' of your likes and dislikes. It will summarize and analyze your strengths for you. He further explores the concept that you are energized when you use your strengths. You would never burn out on a job that uses your strengths.

Winning Strategies Advice in Action: Finding Your Strengths
"I am almost finished reading your book, which has been awesome!, and I just got the strength finders book today. I actually finished the quiz, and I'm VERY surprised at what strengths it identified. I read the whole strengths report, and focused in on my specific five strengths - what an incredible learning opportunity." A. .D., London, England

*Many people that take the quiz are surprised! ~
Bethany*

**Key Point: To Avoid Burnout, Find Your Strengths
and Use Them.**

**Find your strengths. If you don't already know
your core strengths, go to www.strengthfinder.com
and find them. If you have people reporting to you,
consider asking them to find their strengths as well.**

Competition from others becomes less noticeable when you
are utilizing your strengths. You have a gift in these areas.
Find the strengths within you and use those strengths to
stand out from the crowd.

My teenager began wondering about her gifts as she
selected a career. She was entering college and wasn't quite
sure what she wanted to do with her life. Don't we all feel
like that sometimes? Of course, we don't have the
advantage of rolling back the clock to when we were 18.
You may be surprised to discover that your children's
strengths are quite different from yours. You can't assume
that they will have similar strengths. Strengths are not
learned. They are innate; they are inborn, natural, and
instinctive. Like a seed in a watermelon, they are within
you from the beginning of your life. They make you
distinct. You are unique and different from anyone else.

Elizabeth, a mentee, was able to identify her strengths by listing out the projects or activities that she had done in the last five years that she enjoyed the most. We then reviewed the list to determine the similarities and characteristics of those activities. They had a common theme of project management. Each of the activities that she enjoyed doing resulted in her ability to see the results. They also involved interaction with the customers and speaking in front of groups. By evaluating the similarities and characteristics of her most liked activities, we were able to get an idea of her core strengths.

Knowing "what makes you tick," and understanding your unique gifts, is extremely helpful in achieving the next step in your career.

My five Core Strengths are:

1)_____

2) _____

3) _____

4) _____

5) _____

What Activities/Tasks do you enjoy doing?

1)_____

2) _____

3) _____

4) _____

5) _____

Characteristics/Similarities of these activities?

1) _____

2) _____

3) _____

4) _____

5) _____

Common Themes/Strengths:

1) _____

2) _____

3) _____

4) _____

5) _____

Winning Strategies Advice in Action: Finding Your Passion

"Hi Bethany,

I'm starting the process to become a teacher and following my strengths and passions. My last day at my current job is this Friday and I am thrilled. I've been thinking of becoming a science teacher since the beginning of college, but I made it sort of a 'Plan B.' Now, I'm ready to make it a reality! Earlier this year, I started tutoring in an elementary school near my apartment on three mornings a week for an hour—and felt a great joy from it. Through tutoring I found out about the alternative certification program which brings career changers in to teach high-need subjects. I started the program, and I'll be teaching in the high schools. After one year (and upon passing exams and finishing the program), I'll have my teaching certificate.
Cheers,"
Trina W., Dallas, Texas

"Awesome, so glad to see you follow your strengths and move into a role that you were born to live. Often we take the next job that comes along, and forget to closely evaluate what brings us joy and what we are passionate to pursue. I'm proud that you've taken a step to follow your dreams and land in a position that allows you to live the life that you are dreaming of. Best Wishes." ~ Bethany

Chapter 1 "Confidence Building" Summary of Key Points:

- Don't let your confidence be swayed
- Think of yourself as a product
- Trust and believe in yourself
- Learn ways to motivate yourself
- Find your strengths and use them

Chapter Two

2. Packaging Yourself: Your Image and Your Brand

Success Dresses Differently

Successful people really do present themselves differently. They look "pulled together." Their hair is styled; their makeup is on. They are attentive to detail. Their appearance alone gives you confidence that they can get the job done. They are able to present themselves professionally and create a look that screams, "I can do it!" Success dresses differently. However, you don't have to take a second mortgage on your house to dress professionally.

Nice business attire can be picked up at thrift stores, or you can slowly build your wardrobe over the course of a few months. As your career advances, you can have more fun with it. Early in your career, you can shop at the second-hand stores. Much later in your career, you can fly to Italy for your suits. Buying suits from Italy is definitely one of my favorite things. It gives me added confidence when walking into a business meeting. Depending upon the pressure of the meeting, and the stress I might feel at the time, I select the 'Milan suits' to add confidence to my walk and presentation.

When I was in my twenties, my mentor candidly told me that I would not get the promotion that I desperately wanted. She advised me that the current way I dressed and wore my hair was holding me back. Frankness, while difficult to find in any mentoring relationship, should be valued. It is a priceless commodity. Many women wear what is handy. They judge what to wear based on the majority of the others in the office. We often avoid dressy attire. Suits and dressy attire can improve your image and change the perception others have about you at work.

My image was barring my capabilities, or hiding the brilliance underneath. Your image can hide your brilliance. The way you look can either move you up the ladder to success or keep you down. Recognize that both your skills AND your image will work together to catapult you to success. It will better your chances for getting a promotion. In other words, changing your image works!

Key Point: A Put-together Image Gives Others Confidence.

The appearance of a successful woman gives others confidence that they will get the job done.

When it comes to your look, often you will need to conform to the opinions of others until you reach a certain point in your career—the point where you have proven yourself. Once there, you have the ability to be freer with your appearance. It seems that, for women, a 'healthy and fit' image is important to rise to the upper levels of corporate America. In short, you will have more freedom in your appearance after you achieve a certain level in your career.

On a bright, sunny afternoon in June, I was returning from the mailbox. My daughter was at the door ready to rake through the pile of mail with me. A periodical had arrived with an article that I had written. We peered over the pages and read every word, which is a bit silly since I wrote the article and my daughter, Heather, and I had read it at least a hundred times before. At the end of the article, my daughter broke out into sheer laughter. I wasn't quite sure what she found so funny, until I saw the picture. The editor or whoever represented the publication had used photo editing software to trim my hair. For months, my clients joked with me about my new hair style. Needless to say, others will try to shape you into what they believe you should be. I couldn't help but wonder why they don't add hair to the bald men who get published. Truth be told, the public will be harder on you than they are on your plump, overweight, bald, male counterparts. Why, you say? I don't rightly know. I can just tell you to expect it, and to grin and bear it.

Winning Strategies Advice in Action: Image
"Dear Bethany,
I have really enjoyed your website. I want to know your secret to being a beautiful, intelligent, successful woman. I have found recently that my looks and age have been a fault to my success. You are a real inspiration to me and I enjoy reading your blog and daily message. Thank you for the inspiration. Sincerely," E. S., San Diego, CA

"Always glad to provide motivation. I never imagined when I started the blog years ago, that it would end up providing inspiration to thousands of women (and men) around the world. Thank you for reading." ~ Bethany

Packaging

"Dressing the part" also entails packaging. Our image makes up a part of our brand. How we package ourselves aids or restricts us in our upward mobility. Many women get braces as adults, just for cosmetic reasons. To be successful, to rise to the top of a company as a professional woman, we must concentrate on our appearance. They say that makeup is a must if you present in front of audiences, but it is also nice to have for everyday business. Every market and organization is different. My advice is to watch the successful women in your organization and follow their lead. Some day you will be the leader, and then you can set the precedence.

Key Point: Image is Part of your Brand.

Your image is part of your brand. It is part of the 'package' that ensures your upward mobility and job retention.

The actress from the show, "Fat Actress," wrote an article about the unfairness between male and female comedians: they expect the male comedians to be fat and unsightly, while expecting the female comedians to be trim, slim, and attractive. This same anomaly seems to exist in the business world. For men, it doesn't really matter how unsightly one is; bosses seem to see through all that straight to the job they get done. Unfortunately, that doesn't always seem to be the case for female executives. Eating right, exercising, and staying youthful and vibrant, or keeping a young look as best you can isn't the worst prescription, is it?

Nancy is a female employee in her fifties who smokes. It appears that she doesn't have her teeth cleaned regularly. The stains are viewable in conversation. She has excellent dental coverage and her cleanings are free. For her, I suggested that she take time off from work, just an hour or so, and take care of herself. She scheduled a cleaning.

The only thing that should stop you from dental work, or medical visits, is a lack of insurance or lack of money. Take the time for your health – it's important! This also applies to those of you that have put off your much-needed mammography visits or annual physicals. Call and make your appointments now. Your body is more important than your job. You leave behind a sign that tells others that you are either heading for success or not heading for success. A body that hasn't been cared for can limit your steps up the ladder.

Avoid Telling All

People you meet can be somewhat judgmental. Human nature leads people to form opinions of you based on what they learn about you. It is usually best to keep most of your personal business just that—personal. They don't really need to know how many times you've been married, or divorced. It doesn't benefit them to know the details about your legal problems, or information about your living situation. It will be important to guard carefully the information that you share at the office.

Key Point: Avoid Telling All.

A component of your image consists of what you say. Avoid revealing too much personal information at the office. Create the image of an 'I have it all together' woman.

◆ ◆ ◆ ◆ ◆ ◆

Try not to air personal information too soon, if you do choose to share personal information. It is important to share it only with those very close to you after an appropriate time period. I once had a new female boss that joined several of us for lunch the first week of her employment. During that lunch, she told us that she was raped as a girl and that her daughter was a product of that rape. We were speechless.

What would you think of someone who shared that information? Would you trust their judgment in front of a customer? You don't share this type of information in the workplace because it can make people uncomfortable. It does nothing to contribute to productivity. It does not increase sales, decrease operating costs, or build your image as a competent professional. Save this type of discussion for your friends, or for your colleagues after you've established a strong working relationship, or maybe never. It will be your call.

SmartPhones and All Those "Little Extras"

Some time ago, I remember being extremely impressed by a Vice President of Marketing that pulled out her digital calendar. It was before they were so common. Now everyone that we work with carries digital accessories. They say something about you. How automated is your work-life? How well do you manage your technology use? When mentoring women, I suggest you make it a point to have up-to-date digital accessories, even if your company doesn't purchase them for you.

Key Point: Use Digital Accessories to Improve Your Productivity.

Your goal is to become more productive with your time, and develop a deep understanding of current communications and other digital accessories developed to aid executives in their career journeys.

Remember, you are building a brand, an image. Your goal is to become more productive with your time. You want to ensure that you understand the current communication and other gadgets swooping in to invade your executives' time. I'm not saying that you can't advance up the corporate ladder with a pen and pad of paper. I'm simply saying that you want to stand out from the crowd. You want to have the best time-management skills. You want to ensure that you are electronically savvy.

Remember that you are creating your brand. Image is important: what you say, how you look, AND what you carry. Do you use a professional looking briefcase? Do you carry a less-than-attractive purse? All of these impact your brand and either cause others to have confidence in you or have a perception that you are less than professional and unable to get the job done.

Key Point: Carry Professional Accessories.

Monitor what you carry (i.e., backpack, briefcase, type of purse).

Chapter 2 "Packaging" Summary of Key Points:

- **Put together an image that gives others confidence**
- **Your image is part of your brand: 'package' your look to ensure upward mobility**
- **Create a 'have it all together' image by watching what you say**
- **Use gadgets and electronics to improve productivity**
- **Positively affect your brand by buying and carrying professional-looking accessories**

Chapter Three

3. The Three Pillars to Establish Your Value

What Does Success Look Like at Your Company?

Success doesn't occur without intimate knowledge of what 'success' looks like for your company. Most organizations post publicly within the company the annual goals and the objectives by which they will accomplish them. Each of those objectives is assigned to an executive in your organization. They are ultimately responsible for carrying through those initiatives and therefore ensuring the company's success. Even if you work in the mail room, you need to understand these initiatives. No job within the company, if you are REALLY looking to advance, is capable of avoiding this responsibility. Every position in the company is ultimately there to pursue the objectives set by senior leadership. Knowledge of these initiatives will be crucial as you move forward in your career. Consider printing them out and taping them up on your desk next to the picture of your reward for your next promotion. These will be helpful to you as you work with the VPs and leaders in your organization to accomplish initiatives.

Ultimately, if you follow these three pillars of value, success is guaranteed. The three pillars of value are:

- o Business & Operational Value
- o Value to the Sales Team and
- o Value to the Customers

Ensure that you are delivering on these three pillars of value. They are measureable by management and they supersede acquisitions, mergers, bosses you don't like, political powerhouses, and office politics. If you can concentrate on the three pillars of value, it will increase your chance of having the position you desire and rising in the corporate structure despite changes that come along the way. Read on for a thorough review of how to add value for your organization in these areas.

Pillar I: Business & Operational Value

Providing value to your organization is a critical component of success. Have you ever really thought about what action items you could act on to improve the business and or operational value in your company? Many employees believe that they cannot make a difference; they believe that things are what they are. They see "issues" all around, yet conclude that it isn't their position or job to suggest changes or to affect that area of the business.

I am not necessarily asking you to step outside of your area. I'm asking you to evaluate your area and level of responsibility and evaluate how they impact the organization. Are there areas that are lacking that interrelate to your area of responsibility? Are there ideas that you have that could really improve the organization if the right got that information?

I once talked to Tara who was fearful of losing her job. She was in her late twenties, and worked in a department with one other full-time employee. Her efforts weren't visible because they were mostly external. Her position concentrated on partnerships with external companies. It would have been hard for executives to know if the work coming out of that area was from her or her male counterpart. The positions included sales communication and the Sales department was struggling with messaging. I suggested she attend some sales demonstrations to see first-hand how the sales team was struggling. If the Sales department is having trouble selling the solution that you are responsible for, it is your responsibility to understand the problem better than anyone else. Once you have a better understanding of the problem, you may be able to assist in the solution. Own the problem. Sometimes you are just waiting for permission. As women, I think we often wait for permission. Well, consider this your permission. You have permission to figure out critical business and operational needs in your area. You have permission to make a list. You then are responsible to look at the list and determine which of those areas you may be able to address. Test the waters with your leadership. Discuss the items on your list. Do you see any consistent themes? Do you find consensus with your peers?

◆ ◆ ◆ ◆ ◆ ◆

Key Point: Figure Out Critical Business and Operational Needs.

Once you have a better understanding of the problem, create solutions that you can propose to your organization. Be a part of the solution.

◆ ◆ ◆ ◆ ◆ ◆

She either didn't want to take that step, or she was resolved that her days were numbered. She had accepted failure. She didn't make an attempt to understand the business or operational issues that the organization was facing in third-party partnerships. After a few months, she was laid off. At the point when problems are recognized, you can take steps to redirect your fate. It's only too late the day after you're "let go." You always have a chance to start anew. She also would have benefited from a lesson in advertising her accomplishments. We will cover that in Chapter 11. Raising awareness of your accomplishments is critical to establishing value for yourself. Your position may be at risk if the organization cannot easily see the benefit that you provide the company. To make changes to the business and operational needs, you need only to take the first step: make a list of areas in which you can participate in problem resolution.

Your list can be simple. Below are a few examples.

Business or Operational Issue   Affects/Causes

1. New competition from XYZ Company **Affects** Sales/profitability
2. No defined process for X process **Causes** Delays in hiring process
3. Implementations is experiencing increasing workload that **Affects** customer satisfaction and timeliness of software installs.
4. Process Z in Y Department **Causes** employees across the organization to not accomplish as much as they can.

_____

_____

_____

Pick at least one item from the list. See if you can come up with ideas on how the company might solve that dilemma. Are there areas where you could suggest ideas to make it better? If so, try it!

You should bring possible solutions to your boss, not problems. Consider taking to your boss only problems where you have some documented solutions. Your boss is there to advise you between solution A, B, or C if you are having trouble deciding. He/She is not there to solve the problems for you. They can also escalate your suggestions throughout the organization. Help your department/area to thrive.

Key Point: Marry Solutions to the Problems You Identify.

Take solutions to your boss *WITH* the problems that you identify. Consider writing up a short proposal for a solution that the organization is facing.

You can stand out by writing a short proposal for a solution to a problem that the organization is facing outside of your area of responsibility. That proposal can be copied and delivered to two or three leaders in your organization. Usually, it is a good idea to give it to your boss and to the executives two levels above him/her. You want to be noticed by more than just your boss, but you also don't want to skip over him/her.

Addressing business or operational value is a great way to always have a job. Companies need thought leaders. They desperately need problem solvers. Women are wired to be great problem solvers. Oftentimes we are stifled in the work place. We believe that we should sit back and let the 'more experienced' ones solve the problems. We wait for permission. That is the wrong way to think about it. In order to run the course, to stay at the company for the long haul (until YOU are ready to leave THEM), you have to help solve their operational problems. It is a sure way to stay employed and to move up.

Pillar II: Value to the Sales Team

If your company sells a product or service, the Sales team is a valuable resource to the company. They can seem time consuming, but they are VERY important to the progress and future of the company. Think of your relationship with Sales as a contract. There are service-level agreements that should be kept. You want to provide a value to the sales team that stands out above and beyond the rest of the people they interact with.

Try this for at least ninety days: Every time a sales representative contacts you, respond as soon as possible. Make it your goal to respond within two hours. Try to go above the service that they would get from anyone else. If you are not responsible for the area in which they have approached you, volunteer to find them the information and get back to them.

You want to be so valuable to the sales team, that they couldn't imagine working at the company without you there. The information you get to them is likely for customer consumption. Think of that when you are formatting or preparing data for them. It will need a cover sheet, with logos, etc. It will need to be in language that could go directly to a customer. Sales personnel talk. They talk to senior leadership regularly. They will be appreciative of the work you do. You will stand out and be noticed. This, I promise.

Key Point: Become a Key Resource to the Sales Team!

You want to provide a value to the sales team that stands above the rest of the people with whom they interact.

Create an informal network of information.

◆ ◆ ◆ ◆ ◆ ◆

If there are graphs or screen shots to describe an answer that you are preparing for sales, then include them. PowerPoint is a great tool to combine images and layer screen shots. PowerPoint makes it easy to overlay pictures or screen shots, grouping them together to form a presentation-level report cover or image that can be imbedded into a MS Word document. A textual description can follow. By creating customer-facing documents when necessary, you become a valuable resource to the sales team.

Keep a copy of anything that you have prepared for sales. It is a great idea to share this with the proposal team or marketing team. Make it your mission to become a resource. Try to know where the information is kept in the company. Where is the collateral that describes what your area of the business does? Is there a way that you could become knowledgeable about where the information is kept, both in files, in employee's heads, and in soft and hard copies? It is a bit of a tightrope, in that some will feel like you are treading on their roles or trying to outdo them. Usually, staff cut backs and downsizing efforts have left many organization's short-staffed. Most personnel that you will interact with won't have a lot of extra resources to continually worry about such things, most of the time. It is possible that you will face negativity. Do not let it deter you; your main goal is to create a differentiating brand for yourself.

However you do it, becoming a valuable resource to the sales team always pays off. It will provide you with opportunities for advancement, increases in pay, and a better chance of avoiding layoffs. You also will learn to see things from the client's perspective. Things look differently from that angle. Being able to do so is a valuable tool to help your organization succeed. Many began to look a blind eye on the way the company 'feels' and 'looks' to a new customer. Like a frog in a boiling pot of water, they don't realize how hot the water is. (I must admit, I don't fully follow the frog analogy. The water is what? Customer service? Or, sales?) They were exposed to the water when it was cold and slowly brought to boiling. Many began to be blind to the outside view of the company. This valuable viewpoint will enable you to become a problem solver and witted solution employee that people will seek out when they have a dilemma that they cannot solve. This (asset) will become a part of your brand.

Pillar III: Value to the Customers

The third pillar is value to the customers. This is the third ring in the trilogy of success. Always invest in your customers. It is always worthwhile to get to know the customers. Share your contact information whenever you get a chance. Offer to follow up when possible, even if you have the information handy when you meet with them. Following up in a day or so with the information will give you a second chance to make an impression. Customer emails and voice mails should get the highest priority. Many have told me, "but I am not on the sales team, I don't need to form relationships with the customers." I disagree.

36

It is imperative to form relationships with the customers. They will give you a perspective that you may not find within the company. They also will provide stable input for you in your career.

Being resourceful and helpful to the customers will pay off over time. You want them to know you. You don't need permission to get to know customers nor do you have to be in any certain position. If you are meeting customers or just sitting in on a presentation, a couple things are very important. Walk around the room before the meeting and greet anyone there. Shake their hands and participate in small talk. It will break the you/them barrier that may exist after the meeting starts. Above all else, stand out. Ask them questions about themselves and their positions. Ask for business cards. Build a network, keeping those business cards in electronic format. In the future, it will be easy to tap into this network when you need to.

Key Point: Invest in Your Customers.

Time spent investing in your customers always pays off.

Treat customers like they are paying your wage. Of all the advice you may read in this book, I think this one has been the most valuable to many women's careers. Treat them like they will decide whether or not you get your next raise or promotion. Many times in my career, when bosses have come and gone, the customers have been the steady feedback loop into the company that has ensured my continued employment. In your business, the customer leadership will most probably keep the same position for much longer than the middle and top management team at your company. In small industries, the customer may move on to become your next boss.

You can provide value to the customers because you know the company better than others that sit outside the four walls. Most companies are complex, difficult to maneuver, and information is at a premium. Often it is difficult for customers to know who to go to when they need something. You can become a resource, routing them to the correct contact person within the company. It will surprise you when you see the results of this labor. I call it "caring for the customers." Make it personal. Make it your responsibility to find one contact from every meeting you attend with customers. Your network and visibility will grow quickly.

Visibility is key in this arena. If you know that someone in your department cannot make a customer-facing meeting, volunteer for it. Remember, you own a brand: it's YOU. Without visibility for that brand, it is not as valued. Make yourself visible. In doing this, provide value to the customers. They have something that your company may not have: long memories and, more importantly, loyalty and trust. They like consistency and will provide value to your career.

Key Point: Be Customer-facing Whenever Possible.

Visibility is key. Customers have something that your company or bosses may not always have: long memories and, more importantly, loyalty and trust.

If they ask you if they can ever do anything for you, this is not a good time to be humble. As women, we lack much in this area. Say, "Yes, you could let my boss/direct supervisor know what you think." Here is more brand management advice: The more your boss/direct supervisor gets compliments on you, the less likely it is that you will be downsized and the more likely that you will be promoted and achieve those much-desired assignments. This will help you define your brand both internally and externally.

These three pillars of value will provide untold benefits in your career. Keep this chapter as a reference to reread from time to time. Remembering these points will help you take the next step.

Chapter 3 "Establish Your Value" Summary of Key Points:

- Success is guaranteed if you are providing value in three key areas:

    1. Business and Operational Value
    2. Value to the Sales Team
    3. Value to the Customers

- Figure out critical business and operation needs
- Marry solutions to the problems you identify
- Become a resource to the sales team
- Invest in your customers
- Be customer-facing whenever possible to raise awareness of your brand

Chapter Four

4. Insider Company Tips

Getting to Know the Company

Whether you are new at your job or not, there are pockets of information that you can tap into. There are wise ways to attack the same old problems in different ways. This chapter will address shining new light on age-old problems. It will address how to pull innovation, creativity, and problem solutions out of your company and your group. By identifying the 'how', you will be able to lead your group and your company forward.

At age 31, I was asked to lead a product line that had been, albeit briefly, sunsetted. It was a visionary product that was years ahead of its time. Competitors had come into the market. Many were trying to build what we already had built. Staff had quickly exited the product area after a merger, once the sunset was official. It felt a bit like getting a ticket to go for a cruise on the Titanic. The key to any good leadership position is the people in the company that support you. I originated on the side of the company that had bought, or merged, with the smaller company. To them, I was perceived as the enemy. Perceptions, however, can be changed.

I had little knowledge of the functional capabilities of the product line and -- although I had visited several customers for the "customer perspective" -- I still *desperately* needed the 'voice of reason.' In Six Sigma definitions, there is the Voice of the Customer, the Voice of the Business, and there should be one more: the Voice of Reason. The Voice of the Customer is a term used to define the customer needs.

The Voice of the Business is the term used to define the business needs. The Voice of Reason is a term I coined for a company reality check. Without it, every idea, every proposal, every thought is really just a *proposed* plan. How do you really know that it will work? Or succeed? Without the Voice of Reason—that valuable internal company advice from the experts throughout the organization—YOU REALLY DON'T KNOW!

Therefore, you must enlist others. I began to identify key resources in the organization that could aid in my quest. These resources do not have to be in leadership. In fact, it's better (best?) if they are not. Seek the most knowledgeable employees in each area that are not in leadership. Find the passionate souls that work like hell to further the cause of your organization. In my organization, I found five, my personal 'Big Five.' (I work in finance, so I named them after the 'Big Five' accounting firms.) All decisions and proposals went by these five key players before I would propose the plan to senior leadership. After two years, this list grew to six. I propose that you make a list of knowledgeable resources within your organization. It will prove valuable to you.

Key Point: Identify Key Resources to Aid You Along the Way.

These key resources will provide the "Voices of Reason" that ensures that plans are put into action successfully.

Once identified, these personnel should get your key attention. Emails and contact from your "Voices of Reason" should receive prompt attention. You should take them for coffee, lunch and occasionally dinner. You should give small gifts, when possible, to show that you appreciate their input. You should complement their work in front of their managers and senior leadership. This group will gain strength to push forward the best and the brightest ideas. In my organization, the "Voice of Reason" consisted of the following individuals:

- Key Implementation Resource who once was a customer
- Consultant who once was a customer
- Sales resource who once was the product manager for the application suite that I was to product manage
- Designer who once was a customer
- Programmer that had programmed the original application
- Custom Deployment resource

Whatever your combination, these key resources will give you a thorough Litmus™ test for ideas as they arise in the course of business. Times too numerous to mention, I have discovered that we had already started an initiative, began coding, and then stopped. I could then kick-start an old initiative, dig up all the history, and have half of the program completed simply because key resources had historical data.

Key Point: Enlist *Others* to Understand the Past and Present. You will See Solutions and Form the Future.

Enlisting the help of others will open up your viewpoints to see the best and the brightest ideas across the company.

What Kind of Data are you Looking for?

These key resources are your sight into the past, vision into the future, and understanding of current situations. In order to 'lead,' you need to understand the life blood of the company.

- Are the key resources satisfied? What about others on the team?
- Do processes seem to work?
- What does he/she think of their department? Their job? Their boss?
- What pressures do they face?
- The key is to listen more than you talk! In time, you will begin to be able to give information just as you receive it, but it is important to begin the process by doing a lot of listening.

Research and Evaluate: Understanding the Big Picture

Data and knowledge are powerful. They will help you when problem solving and leading your organization forward. Early in my career, I didn't recognize the power in data and research. Knowing the specifics of the direction of your company and the direction of the market surrounding your industry is crucial to your upward mobility. I was struck by a move AT&T made decades ago. They were heavily invested in copper piping, but the market was quickly moving to fiber optics. In 1989, they made a move, taking a huge hit to the bottom line[i], in an effort to write off as much of the copper piping as possible and move the company forward into newer options. I'm sure it was a tough decision. They took a $3.935 billion dollar hit. Had they not done this, however, they could have been out of business in just a few years.

Someone was obviously doing her research. As corporate women, we need to be in a position to see the market and market forces surrounding our industry. This global view allows us to move upward in the company. We will have a wider view, therefore adding additional value to our viewpoints, ideas, and company directional advice.

The internet makes this much easier. You can find information and articles about topics of interest to your company. I suggest you subscribe to trade publications for your area, nationally or internationally, where appropriate. (Often employers will pay for these.) But, have them delivered to your home address where you might be more likely to peruse them when you have free time.

Even an occasional read of Fortune, Business Week, Money, or the New York Times will help you keep your eyes open to potential market changes that could affect your organization. If you happen to see a potential risk headed toward your company and its profits, than it's your obligation to think about solutions to mitigate that risk.

These are great opportunities to call a meeting with the CEO or senior management. (Chapter 12 discusses communicating with senior management, i.e., your CEO.) The research and knowledge you gain will help you as you begin to take on "company thinking."

Reading the annual report if you are a public company is a good idea too. What is your organization telling the market that the company's goals and objectives are? What is the expected revenue growth? If you were the owner, what would you want to know?

What about trends? Are there some that you should be watching? Are some businesses outsourcing your department work to India? Is your organization's product less competitive in the market (cars, for example).

What are Your Competitors Doing?

Valuable information about YOUR company lies in the realm of knowledge regarding your competitors. For the first several years of my career, I concentrated solely on my employer. Little did I know that looking only inside my company's four walls left valuable information undiscovered that was necessary to the success of the company, and to my climb up the corporate ladder.

As with relationships, concentrating solely on what is inside the walls of your company (or your house, in the analogy), leaves you vulnerable to what affects you from the "outside."

◆ ◆ ◆ ◆ ◆ ◆

Key Point: Keep a Vigilant Eye on the Competition.

Evaluating the competition will help you become a thought leader. It will enable you to become a resource to the company and help ensure the company's future success.

You cannot understand the business in total unless you closely evaluate the competition. I struggled intensely in sales until I figured out this valuable skill: Many answers are revealed when you learn about the competition. Often your competitors will announce their moves in press releases (if they are a public company), or in advertisements. Regional trade shows are also a great source for gleaning competitive data. In some industries, there are experts that offer reports on the market and the competition, for a fee. Gartner is an example of one of these companies. If they are not producing press releases, advertisements, or publishing articles, than this data is very hard to come by. But, it is still important. It usually takes a company years to operationalize a stated direction, so you can gather this information slowly over time. Sometimes researching the job market also enables you to discover what the competition is doing.

About thirteen years into my career, I discovered that the company I was working for was about to make a decision that went directly against the movement of most of our competitors. This I took note of. It was a significant data point. It caused further research and evaluation of the competition. Why was the entire market moving one way, and our company moving another? If it wasn't by design, would it prove to be an error? If you have done your homework, it's rather easy get an audience with senior

47

executives to share your research and suggested solutions. Well thought out research and strategy is hard to come by. It is unusual for someone to make an outspoken request to share research data that could positively affect the future of the company. You just added value to your brand!

It was at this point in my career that I begin to better see the big picture. When competitive forces were factored in with market forces, the picture that was my company's operations looked much different than it had just months before. I begin to understand what was standing in the way of our company meeting our goals and objectives.

I begin to think through how we could mitigate these risks, even in my department. I felt the connection to the overall health and wellness of the company. I begin to see exactly how I could stand out and make global change at my company. You can do this too.

A couple of years later, my thinking expanded even further. I moved from the me-too competitive thinking into a mind set of "getting there first." That moment is cemented in my career's history.

If you begin to deeply understand the forces facing your organization, you will begin to add a greater level of value than other employees. You will find yourself suggesting new service offerings and objectives that match or exceed your competition. The words you use and the way you speak will change. You will have more input when asked. You're brand is working!

You can start by writing out a small project to identify three to four of the top competitors in your market space. Then, you identify key areas about each of them:

- ✓ Current Positions
- ✓ Strategic Direction
- ✓ Differentiators
- ✓ Competitive Strengths
- ✓ Competitive Weaknesses
- ✓ Company Customer Base
- ✓ Product/Service Offerings
- ✓ Technology Used
- ✓ Public/Private/or Funded
- ✓ Financial Position

You will be amazed at how much information you can glean from publicly available data. You can begin to watch closely for ad campaigns, articles on the competition, and market reports. I advise you to become the expert on the competition. I guarantee you will move up in the ranks!

The Art of Clear Communication

Ever realize that each generation is wielding a new tool kit of thinking and computer skills. The younger generations think differently. They solve problems differently. They react to things differently. Compound this with our ability to make things overly complex, and we miss the most basic in-your-face benefit or view. This is why depending on your son, daughter, neighbor, or nephew is a great idea. Run the idea or opinion by them. You will be surprised at the response.

I was amazed when I began to run software prototypes by my then eight-year old son, Brandon, and my then fifteen-year old daughter, Heather. Their perspectives, both varied, were very helpful in an evaluation. Have you ever seen the same thing for so long that you see it skewed? Well, that is actually quite common. It is why you should always take vacation time. A fresh look at something is a great idea, even if that fresh look is you just back from the Bahamas.

Our children began working with computers in Kindergarten, or before. They have grown up with cordless phones, cell phones, and Playstation™ games, They inherently abide by different rules than we do. They think differently.

This will teach you the important skill-set of being able to explain your ideas, concepts or thoughts in a simple, easy-to-understand way. The problem statements should be simplistic. The answer should be even easier to state. If you practice explaining your concepts in simple language, you will learn a valuable skill. You will learn to state the problem and the solution simplistically. This skill-set prepares you for explaining it to senior leadership. I am not at all saying that they need simple terms to understand. I'm saying that we add too many details and too much information for the message to be clear. After explaining it to the youngsters in your life, you will begin to understand how to explain it to others. It is a valuable skill-set that you will be glad you learned.

Finding the Company Historians

It is amazing how many times companies will repeatedly attempt the same task, each time getting the same results. What are they thinking? Well, I have discovered that somewhere buried deep within the company are "company historians." These are the personnel that know exactly how many times the company has tried this or that. They also know the result of each attempt. They know the lessons learned. The only problem is that the 'lessons learned' are not juxtaposed with the current decisions being made, perhaps because these "historians" hold positions that do not communicate with senior leadership.

I advise you to find these company historians. They will have been with the company for numerous years. They will be in positions where they can fly under the radar. Your goal is to befriend someone in this category.

I worked for 10 years at a hospital group in San Diego. My mentor, Karen, and I knew the company history well. It was amusing for us to try to name the last year that the company had tried to reorganize or implement a "new," yet similar, plan previously. The company was repeating the same mistakes. Each time, a few years in between marked enough time for a new set of senior leaders to emerge who were unaware of the past decisions. They would launch their *new* ideas, hoping to solve age-old problems. There is nothing wrong with trying the same plan twice. It just makes more sense to research the reason that the plan didn't succeed the first time.

Once you have tapped into the resources of the company historians, you will be girded with the knowledge of past successes and failures. You can delicately use this information to help guide your boss and the senior leaders of the company toward better decisions and better outcomes. I suggest you avoid disagreeing with the ideas that your boss or senior leader has. Consider offering consultative assistance. How would you apply the concept? It could go this:

Boss: We will be re-organizing X department into such-and-such teams.
You: I heard that we re-organized X department in Y year. It didn't succeed then, but most put the blame on a lack of a good strong leader to lead it through and enough empowerment to wield the results necessary.
Boss: Great input. I hadn't heard that. Who led that initiative then?
You: (name)
Boss: Hmmm, I was planning to put him in charge of this re-organization as well. I may have to think this through a little more.

Your end goal is company success. This tip is to help your company learn from its mistakes, by finding information about the past (if you weren't there then) and openly sharing that information in a positive way.

This can help tremendously if you are new to the company. It can be your key to solving the most difficult problems. You can use several data points to guide you to a great solution. The data points to evaluate are as follows:

- ✓ What history exists about the topic/problem/solution?
- ✓ Has it ever caused the company to lose a sales deal?
- ✓ Have solutions been created that no one would approve?
- ✓ Have customers solved it without the company's assistance?

- ✓ Is there documentation anywhere on the topic within the company?
- ✓ Is there documentation anywhere on the topic outside of the company?

These data points, and the meetings with company historians, will give you a chance to rummage through information and find the priceless pieces. You then will be able to apply these pieces of information upward as opportunities allow. This ability can help you establish yourself as a thought leader in the company. You will always acknowledge your sources of data, but having the big picture and knowing the past missteps will help you to build your brand.

Brainstorming

To be valuable, you need to be a thought leader. Organizations always have more problems than solutions, more difficulties than plans. To be most valued, you should lead the process for the organization that will extract the solutions to the toughest problems they seek. Once extracted, you can document and lead the organization to solve these dilemmas.

Businesses' problems can feel like big impenetrable mountains. I remember when an invasive regulatory demand came out. There was a possibility that the programming wasn't going to be done in time to meet the regulatory deadline. Just the thought of such a huge failure in my area caused my heart to race and my blood pressure to rise. So, when you are faced with a big dilemma or potential problem, what do you do?

Often, large dilemmas require one of two things, sometimes both:

1. **Data Gathering exercise** - Gather all the details/facts that you can. This may require several touch points with personnel in the organization. This *will* require customer contact, in that customer expectations need to be closely identified. Document all data obtained. Keep good record. It will help you with decision making.
2. **Brainstorming exercise** - In order to have a healthy brainstorming exercise, you will need to either be a good facilitator, or invite one to the meeting. The goal will be to try to 'draw out' some proposed solutions to the dilemma that you are facing. Be prepared to throw out a couple of wild ideas to get their creative juices flowing.

   In our brainstorming exercise, we discovered abilities to role (rule? roll?) out software rules that could solve the regulatory dilemmas until official software code could be rolled out in deployment. I began to have these brainstorming sessions every 4 to5 months. As regulatory changes were coming fast and furious, these allowed us to throw out all the ideas and move forward in the direction that the group advised.
3.

Key Point: Use Data Gathering and Brainstorming to Solve Impenetrable Problems

Gather all the details and facts that you can, then facilitate a brainstorming exercise with a cross functional team. You may need several sessions to solve the dilemma.

Sources of Negative Data - a Gold Mine

Important in the ability to lead an organization is to understand the climate of the organization. When organizations are unhappy, they grumble. Grumbling organizations are not productive. If you listen, you can hear company difficulties coming before they hit. Ever walk into a room and feel the thickness in the air. One day during a meeting, someone from customer support said, "Let the customer go to the competitors, see if I care." Usually a comment like this is indicative of a much larger problem. They may have a work load that is too large, or they may be missing key resources necessary to do their job. There may be a difficult boss situation, or even a complex personal situation. The organization may have cut back staff, and they may be left with way too much work. Those are good questions for leadership.

Key Point: Negative Comments Can Be Indicative of Bigger Organizational Problems.

Employees may have a workload that is too large, they may be missing key resources or training necessary to do their job, or there may be a difficult boss situation.

The conversation to senior leadership should go something like this. Do you think we have enough staff in customer support? The answer could come back, "Yes, we are fully staffed."

You: "I heard a staff member make a very negative comment and was just wondering if her team was understaffed." You could then share the comment.

Senior Leader: "Who said that?"

Never reveal your source; you will need them again. They are usually not the problem, just a sign that there are problems.

You: "I'd rather not say...I just thought that it may be indicative of a broader problem in support for that application/area."

As it turned out, that particular product area was understaffed at the time. Had I revealed the name of the person that said the comment, it wouldn't have improved the root of the problem. It would have only made matters worse. Don't reveal your negative sources of data. Knowing the information is more powerful than revealing your source. However, positive sources of data are entirely different animals. Always recognize their contributions. Read on.

◆ ◆ ◆ ◆ ◆ ◆

Key Point: Keep Your Sources Confidential.

By keeping your sources confidential, you will be trusted in the organization. Staff will not feel like they have to tip toe around you. You will begin to see and hear things that the others in leadership do not see and hear. You then will be able to truly lead.

Recognizing Contributors

A consistent theme that should be shooting off the page is the fact that it takes a village to lead and to succeed. It takes a village of supportive, encouraging, and proficient staff to help you to the top. You will need to recognize the contributions of those that assist, support, and continuously aid you in your trek to the top of the hill. I suggest you make a point to recognize those that contribute to the projects in which you participate. If someone gave you information, be sure to mention their name in the presentation verbally, or in written format for written proposals. It is imperative that all sources be recognized adequately. Emails should say, "considerable thanks to the following individuals without whom I could not have accomplished this:"…then list them.

I cannot tell you how many times in my career someone has taken my work and put their name on it. Many of those times, they also received bonuses and additional compensation for my work. We cannot change that it happens, we can only ensure that we do not contribute to it. It is still an irritant in the business world today. You will go further, be promoted faster, and be MORE recognized for your contribution if you recognize the people that gave you information. Recognize the contributors that gave you their research data, their PowerPoint slides, and their input. On the first page of any internal write up, document a section for "Written By:" and your name. Below that section, recognize contributors: Credit them with simple verbiage, such as *with major contribution from:" and their name*. This will ensure that you give credit where credit is due. And, hopefully, others will respect you and your work in the same way.

Key Point: You Will Go Further, Be Promoted Faster, and Be More Readily Recognized for Your Contributions if you Recognize Others.

Make a point to recognize those that contribute to the projects that you participate in. Recognize the people that gave you their research data, information, excel spreadsheets, PowerPoint slides, and their input.

The people you recognize in the organization also will be promoted. Over the years, the 'Voices of Reason' will be promoted and moved up in the organization. One reason for this is that you will be able to recognize their contributions. This will bring light to their accomplishments and value. It will result in their being promoted.

Avoid Becoming a Datamonger: Instead Spread the Love

Probably the most astonishing advice I have for you is this: share! There's a myth in business that says "if I keep data all to myself, then I will become more valuable to the organization." We will call these people the datamongers. They are everywhere. Some of them try to keep everything in their head. They don't want to write anything down. These people are harmful to the forward motion of a company. You cannot climb the corporate ladder and be a datamonger, the two do not go together. You must learn to share. I promise that you will still be valuable and you will still keep your job. This piece of advice requires trust, however..

Key Point: You Cannot Climb the Corporate Ladder and be a Datamonger; the Two do not Go Together.

You must share. You will be more valuable and will create a higher value add and propensity for you to keep your job.

Think of broad ways to share what you have done:
- **Templates:** Did you create a great spreadsheet that could be used by others? Make a template specifically for sharing purposes.
- **Presentations:** Is your PowerPoint™ presentation share worthy? Share it!
- **Visit Notes:** Did you type notes when you were at the customer site? Keep these in a file and store them on the network, if you have a network file location.
- **Notes**: Did you take great notes at a meeting or a training seminar? Share these notes across your department and other departments.

Your goal is to become a valuable resource in your company. You can burn CDs of data for staff in the company. Think of something that you could do that would fill a need in your organization? Carefully think through everything that you document and evaluate its worthiness for sharing. If it is worthy, then keep it in a central location or identified well so that you can easily pluck it out to share. If you are not sharing documents regularly, then you need to re-evaluate the effectiveness of your communication and the quality of the documents you produce.

Remember that plagiarism is truly the best compliment that your co-workers and peers could pay you. Recycling your templates, report covers, or documents shows their worthiness. About four years into adopting this theory, I noticed that I could account for more than one hundred people utilizing templates that I had developed. It grew even beyond that. The data spread and its' usefulness grew.

Key Point: Spread Your Work Throughout the Organization.

The more visible your work, the higher you increase your brand value.

How far can you spread your work throughout the organization? The further it spreads, the more valuable you are to the company. The more visible your work, the higher you increase your brand value.

Chapter 4 "Insider Company Tips" Summary of Key Points:

- Identify key resources in the organization to aid you along the way
- Enlist others to help you understand the past and present, it will help you see solutions and form the future
- Listen more than you talk
- Keep a vigilant eye on the competition
- Use data gathering and brainstorming to solve impenetrable problems
- Negative comments can be indicative of bigger organizational problems
- Keep your sources confidential
- You will go further, be promoted faster, and be more recognized for your contributions if you recognize others
- You cannot climb the corporate ladder and be a datamonger; the two do not go together
- Spread your work throughout the organization to increase your brand value

Chapter Five

5. Turning Problems into Solutions

Move from Complaining to Creating Solutions

A big inhibitor to female success is an aptitude for whining, gossiping and complaining. It falls into a category of non-productive chatter. If we funnel this energy into solving problems, we become strong company assets. Try speaking only when you have a potential solution to recommend. If you don't have a solution, keep the problem to yourself until uou have a thoroughly thought-out solution. This will greatly limit the amount of words that you speak. We need to remain positive. If there are problems, they shouldn't be discussed unless you are participating in a problem-solving discussion. Some of you may take offense that I have even mentioned this, while others are copying this section to leave on the desk of a co-worker. Our goal should be to build each other up, not to cut each other down. Often we don't realize the damage that has been done by voicing our complaints. It paints an image of our brand that isn't positive. It doesn't give the perception that we are leaders and problem solvers.

Key Point: Funnel Your Energy Into Solving Problems to Become a Strong Company Asset.

Avoid whining, gossiping, and complaining. Funnel this energy into solving company problems.

Our male counterparts are terrific at building up their male cohorts, as well as keeping silent about company problems until it is necessary to talk about them. They don't need to talk about them to process them. If you need to discuss the problems, talk to a friend, NOT a co-worker. What if I told you that the habits mentioned in this chapter could keep you from excelling? It could keep you from making much more money than you are making today. Motivate yourself to funnel energy into solving problems and become a strong company asset.

Gossip

Gossip is a dangerous and frightful thing. It is like a serpent with many heads.

The Hydra.

In ancient Greek mythology, the Hydra was a serpent with nine heads. Today, gossip is our Hydra. We don't recognize that simply listening to others gossip makes it appear that we agree with what is being said. There are eight hidden heads to every one we see. We need to avoid association with this monster at all costs. There's no need to appear prudish, simply say, "I have to get to work," and walk away when the gossip begins. Remember, anything that you speak will be repeated. It's likely that the repetition will be back to the person that you were talking about. Before the words flow out of your mouth, think about whether or not you would say those words directly to that person. If not, than the words are better left unsaid.

Key Point: Listening to Gossip Makes it Appear That You Agree With What is Being Said.

It is advisable to avoid association with negative "water cooler" chatter.

Personnel that do not perform will find their way out the door without your gossip. Reserve your opinions for times when superiors ask you for them. Be prepared with concise, non-opinionated statements that reflect the truth. Examples of this would be: "My opinion is that Frank would be better in a less customer facing role. He is defensive at times and it can come across as negative to the clients." Most likely, if Frank has issues with the clients, others would have reported this as well. Our opinions are best saved for direct questions from superiors, never for hallway gossip.

If you disapprove of something Frank did say in a customer phone call, it is always best to take it directly to Frank and speak with him in person. Some wrong ways to handle this would are leaving a voice mail or email, or discussing it with *anyone* other than Frank.

Silence is Acceptance

Few recognize that silently listening is silently agreeing with all you hear. If you are listening to someone say that the VP of the Development area is a witch, than you are silently agreeing, even if she got you your job. You have two choices if you don't agree. You can comment on what you think about her skill-set in a positive way, or you could say "I have to get back to work" and exit the scene.

You must make a decision. Do you want to remain in your current position and pay level, or do you want to move up to the next level? Participating in gossip and inefficient hallway chatter about non-work topics for extended time periods can limit your upward mobility. You either reflect an air of an efficient, busy and effective worker, or you look like you have loose lips and too much time on your hands. Listening to gossip is like a dump truck pulling up and dumping out a load of garbage. No one ever dumps garbage on a nice, neat lawn. They only dump in areas that have awful appearances, like alleys and other trashed-out areas. So, if someone is dumping gossip on your 'lawn,' maybe you should trim the grass and clean up around the edges.

Your Boss: Making Him/Her Look Good

Your boss is on your team. Whether or not you like her, respect her, or feel that she has what it takes it do the job. After all, she is your boss. As part of accepting your paycheck, it is honorable and right to make her look good in any way possible. If she looks bad, you look bad. This attitude can take you to new heights. Find her strengths and bring those out. Help her fill the holes that she is missing. If she is not a detail-oriented person, help her assign someone to that role. Fill some of her gaps by offering to assist her on special assignments. When others ask you what you think of her, always mention positive characteristics. Bring out the best in her. Helping her get ahead is part of your job. If she is not good at what she does, it will come out on its own.

Concentrating on Your Universe

Think of everything in your universe. Picture a large circle drawn on a board. Inside this circle is everything that you will encounter while working on your job.

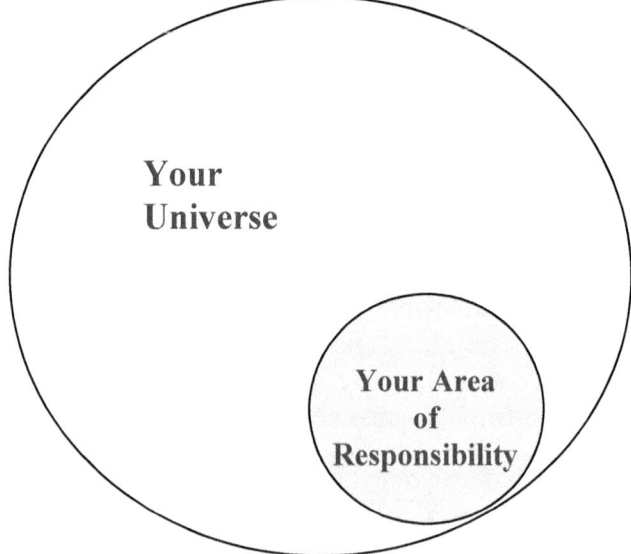

Now picture a smaller circle within the bigger circle. This represents your area of responsibility. The smaller circle represents what you have been hired to do. You are expected to spend eighty percent of your time in this smaller circle. Only ten to twenty percent of your time should be spent in the areas outside of your direct control. These are areas that you can influence but do not directly manage or control. Spending a large amount of time trying to change areas that you do not have direct management or influence over will simply lead to frustration and stress. You are paid to work in the smaller circle. In that area, you are completely responsible for what you have been hired. You need to take charge and accomplish the tasks and goals set out for you in your circle of responsibility.

Key Point: Manage Within Your Circle.

Work to spend 80% of your time in your area of responsibility. Only 10-20% of your time should be spent in the areas outside of your direct control.

Over the years, I have used this drawing and this speech hundreds of times. We often get stuck in frustration over what we cannot change in areas outside of our control, and we lose track of what we can directly affect.

Jake managed the Product Demonstration Team. He was frustrated, and he knew that he was not achieving his goals. My advice, as it turned out, came too late in the game. He rattled on and on about difficulties with the database, getting code from the development organization, and the inability to control the schedules of the demonstration staff.

I pointed out that these were all areas in his 'universe' but not under his direct control. He had been so concerned with the areas that he could not change, he had not concentrated on the things he could change. This is a vicious trap that we fall into. In this situation, he could have:

- Enhanced the professionalism of the team:
  - Prepared bios
  - Ordered name badges
  - Held team-building exercises
- Had weekly calls to listen to and understand their issues
- Facilitate formal processes for getting information on prospects
- Scheduled training

Once he ensured that his area was running smoothly and had all the key ingredients to a professional and fine-tuned area, he could begin to put together a plan for correcting issues with the database and getting code from development. He needed to concentrate on the 80% of his job BEFORE he could begin a project on the other 20%. It wasn't long before he was either let go or asked to leave. Soon after, he was replaced. It wasn't a surprise.

The message is clear. Concentrate on the areas of responsibility that you have been given. Ensure that, in those areas, you are doing everything that you know to do to form a team that is organized, with processes in place to accomplish the tasks and goals of the department. Once you have your area running well, then you can begin to look at areas outside of your direct circle of influence.

Chapter 5 "Turning Problems into Solutions" Summary of Key Points:

- **Funnel your energy into solving problems to become a key company asset**
- **Listening to gossip makes it appear that you agree with what is being said**
- **Manage within your circle of influence**

Chapter Six

6. Attitude is Everything! ... and other Little Rules for Success

What other things hold us back or push us forward? In this chapter, we will review the six things that work to push women forward in the workplace;

1. **Avoid preconceived notions and discriminations**
2. **Show appreciation**
3. **Recognize that everyone can make a difference**
4. **Change your perspective**
5. **Take risks**
6. **Admit when you are wrong**

Avoid Preconceived Notions and Discriminations

An important learning factor is to trust your own judgment and not to believe what you hear about others. Time and again, negative comments about co-workers will be shared with you. These comments can cloud your judgment and keep you from seeing people through your own eyes. It took me several years before I learned to discard most everything that I hear about others. I learned to avoid preconceived notions and to form my own opinions.

Key Point: Trust Your Own Judgment; Don't Believe What You Hear.

Bethany Williams

Learn to see people through your own eyes, form your own opinions, and use your own judgment.

We all have filters that we view information through. When others share their viewpoint, they are filtering the information through filters that have become such a part of their being that they do not recognize them any longer. I have taken over teams of personnel and been advised that I would probably have to fire one of them. She turned out to be my star player. Give everyone a second chance. Make your opinions based on firsthand knowledge, not hearsay. Their flaws may be something that you can work on with them. If you help someone to advance and excel, they will become a great advocate to you in your career. Women compatriots are dependable and loyal. When it comes to helping someone in their career, every good deed does not go undone. The time you spend lending a hand, listening when others need to talk, catching up over coffee, or just believing in them when no one else does will come back to you tenfold.

The more diverse and varied your team is, the better your teams will perform. If you hire or choose to work with others that are exactly like you, you lose valuable input. Every executive team should have a MUCH younger player on the team. Perspective changes when you deal with someone that was using a computer in Kindergarten. Also, if you mix in variations in race and religions, you will get a diverse team that will prove to be strong and productive.

Oftentimes people don't hire extremely qualified candidates because they believe that their own position will be at risk.

They believe that they will be somehow be out shown. You can never be out shown. Hire smart people, you want them to secede you when you move up. You are MORE valuable if you can build strong teams that perform well. If you want to be promoted, then you absolutely must hire someone that could take over your position at some point. If your team performs better than any other team, YOU and your team will stand out.

Key Point: Hire Smart People to Replace You When You Move Up.

Hiring smart people will ensure that there is a capable body to move into your position as you move up.

Show Appreciation

One thing sorely missing in the working world today is appreciation. We quickly admonish people for doing wrong and seem to be slow to show appreciation. Appreciation can help you in an untold amount of ways. It will move mountains you never thought possible. You will see amazing things happen. It is such a simple concept. The simplest things go the furthest. So, what am I suggesting? I am suggesting that you open your eyes wide open. Notice EVERYTHING that others do on your behalf. Give the administrative secretary that setup the meeting for you, a heartfelt thank you. Buy a single stem flower or a bag of M&Ms if you let her know about the meeting at the last minute. If the General Manager's right hand lady got you in for a meeting even though he was fully booked, take her to lunch.

Key Point: Show Appreciation to Others.

Show appreciation through positive verbal comments, buying small gifts, sending appreciation emails, and taking people to lunch.

Treat everyone like they are doing you a favor when they do what you thought yesterday was just 'part of their job'. They truly don't have to go out of their way for you if they don't want to. Make them want to.

Send emails that let people know that you appreciate them, their contribution, and their efforts that were shown for X Customer or Y Meeting. Emails have become such a waste of time these days. Everyone copies everyone on everything. We will cover email communications in a later chapter, but for now, let's just say that probably 0.0007% of those are actually emails that are expressing appreciation, gratitude or pure thanks for a job well done. Make sure that you are expressing appreciation in 1 out of every ten emails that you send out. Use handwritten notes, and stickies to express thanks. Leave a note on their desk with a 'just wanted to thank you, AGAIN, for your help' message.

Two employees helped me tremendously once, when I was struggling with a big account. It was their job to do so, but they didn't have to go above and beyond. Not knowing them well, I decided to send them some chocolate with a thank you note. Each future account that necessitated their assistance was met with a gracious and helpful attitude. They offered their assistance when needed. Employees that are appreciated will work harder to help you along the way. Create a brand that says that you appreciate the help of others. Build a team of followers and helpers to pursue your cause.

To recognize entire teams, consider creativity in your thinking. Recognize teams of people that fight with you. It can be small. This is done so little in businesses today that even the smallest token will stand out above the crowd. It will create a brand that says, I appreciate all that you do even though others may not. Ever have a boss buy you a Christmas gift. Consider purchasing decorative ornaments or candy jars for their desks, to ensure that they know that you greatly appreciated their efforts.

Key Point: Appreciation is a Big Motivator.

Even the smallest token of appreciation will stand out above the crowd.

You cannot excel, or move to the top of any company without a village behind you.

Mary Kay has done an incredible job of doing this. In the company that Mary Kay built, there are incentives and rewards built into the infrastructure and flowing throughout the company. The company uses jewelry, gifts, vacations, and other perks to reward women for achieving and to incent them to do more. And you know what? It works. It works in a big way. There are more female millionaires as a result of Mary Kay than any other company in the world. Appreciation is a big motivator.

It isn't about money; it is about heartfelt appreciation. You cannot excel, or move to the top of any company without a village behind you. They will be the air in your balloon.

You will find immeasurable value in a team that supports you. My team supported me in my role. They were dependable. They worked hard and long hours when the clients were in dire need. They had quick responses when I sent out sales questions, and implementation queries. They showed concern and respect to me and others on the team. Each of them has a heart of gold. I know that without them, I couldn't exceed. Without them, I couldn't excel. The funny thing is that they felt the same way about me. Our mutual respect and admiration was built over time.

This starts with you learning the art of appreciation. There are things that happen every day that you no longer notice. It no longer amazes you when certain things happen. You begin to overlook details because you are so accustomed to them happening. This happens in relationships all the time. We hear people say that they didn't really appreciate someone until they were gone. We don't recognize the contribution of those around us until no one is there to contribute.

Recognize That Everyone Can Make a Difference

The most valuable players in the organization are the ones you will never meet unless you try. They are working in the infrastructure of the organization. There are valuable players at all levels and all areas of the company. I hear employees constantly saying, " I can't make a difference, I am only a _____ (insert whatever title here, Analyst, Clerk, Manager, Director, Call Center Representative, etc.). The most valuable lesson we can ever learn, and can pass along to others that we come in contact with, is that EVERYONE can make a difference. We can make a difference in any position that we find ourselves in. Thinking that we cannot make a difference is dangerous. It limits us. We put boundaries around ourselves. If you believe that you cannot make a difference, than you can't. Our own beliefs actually bar us from achieving great things and making greater pay. Don't let the little voices within that try to talk you out of making a difference in your world, win out.

Key Point: Search Out the Diamonds in the Rough.

Sometimes, the most valuable players are the ones that you will never meet unless you try.

The best way to excel and achieve in your company is to begin making a difference right where you are.

If you are waiting for X title or Y position to make a

difference for the company, you will never get X title or Y position. The best way to excel and achieve in your company is to begin making a difference right where you are. Work on standing out. Try to do the job you have been given better than anyone ever has. Knowing your strengths, as discussed in Chapter 1, will aid you in this regard. It is a great place to start. Pick the parts of your job that you love to do. These are the areas that you will work to excel in. If your strengths are in areas that you cannot really apply to your position, then you can apply for positions that do apply your strengths. Applying your distinct strengths will be the best way for you to stand out and excel. Visualize yourself in a role and go for it. If you want the part, then play the part.

As your brand manager, you must make your brand stand out. You will do this by showing MORE appreciation than others, as well as working to make a bigger difference than others. You will do this by avoiding discrimination and pre-conceived notions. You MUST STAND OUT. In the last chapter, we reviewed the universe that is your job and how to concentrate on that universe. Remember, by limiting the parameter of your focus, you are better enabled to make a big difference in your area of responsibility.

Change Your Perspective

Several years ago I went to Ghana, Africa, on a mission trip. Spending several days in a Third World country changed my perspective. Having spent my entire life in cities and suburbs that have infrastructure, bathrooms, and food, I was seeing the world through rose-colored glasses.

Children walked around without clothes, wondering where their next meal would come from. They had no toys, for the most part. There were a couple of children with a small wheel carved out of wood that they pushed around with a stick. Their entertainment, if they were in the lucky few, was for fifty-plus village kids to ALL share a soccer ball. Disabled children were basically on their own. Blind children didn't have special schools to go to, and the disabled didn't have wheelchairs.

We headed to a village in the innermost parts of Ghana. There were six of us, packed into a small SUV. As we encountered people on the trail (it was really a grassy trail that we were driving on), we would stop and pick them up. We passed by old cars that had been deserted. I guess if it breaks down here, you just get out and walk. Then the grassy road changes directions to route around the broken down car. By the time we arrived in the village, there were about twenty people in the SUV, some hanging out the door. It was funny to us Americans that when asked if there was room, the Ghanians would say, "Sure, lots of room," and we Americans would say, "No, all full." It was really a matter of perspective.

Crammed into an SUV with twenty people, all lacking deodorant and the luxuries of daily showers, I realized that I lived in a kingdom of wealth and plenty. I realized that I have been blessed beyond what I even realized. I recognized that the portraits television painted of wealth and plenty, was really an oversold dream, and that I already lived in my own 'story of the rich and famous.'

I saw very few women my own age, most had died prior to reaching their mid to late thirties. I witnessed villages with no running water, or access to water anywhere nearby. The huts that they slept in had no beds or furniture whatsoever.

Their living huts had one room, with dirt floors and branch roofs. The area was considered 'open range.' This meant that you could squat anywhere to use the bathroom since there were none.

All that the people could talk about constantly, was how great their lives would be if they lived in the United States. It was their promised land. They had seen the pictures, and had lived their entire lives wishing they could live in the states, the great land of plenty. I realized that I could be homeless, and living here on the streets and I would be better off than most of the people that I met in Ghana. In the states, I would have access to healthcare. I would have access to shelters. There would be people that could help me, if I wanted help. I could find running water, and bathrooms. There would be drinking water aplenty. I would not die of Malaria because I didn't have the dollar that it took to buy medication.

Somehow, when I think about my time in Africa, I am brought back to a new reality. I have a changed perspective. I can face situations and circumstances without being jarred into complete frustration. I can look at business frustrations through new eyes. Regardless of how difficult the situation seems, no one is going to die from it. No one will starve to death. People are not losing their lives because we make a bad decision. Or at least, this is true for most of us. I recognize that for some in direct patient care, decisions can affect lives.

Key Point: Create a New Reality and a Changed Perspective for Yourself.

Attempt to face situations and circumstances without being jarred into completed frustration.

Find a new ruler with which to measure your world and the world around you.

My mentoring advice to all of you is to find a new perspective. Find a new ruler with which to measure your world and the world around you. Spend some time donating your time and efforts to charity. Spend a day at the battered women's shelter. Work in the soup kitchen in the downtown area. Volunteer at a pregnancy resource center. This time will be well spent. You will walk away with a changed perspective. You will see your world through different glasses. You will be able to stand tall and make a difference, savoring each little gift that life has in store for you.

My advice on changing perspective is here because we do have a harder road, still than our male counterparts. However, I am not going to focus on the negative, my advice is to strive forward making major steps and accomplishing your goals. Recognize that you are blessed beyond belief. This changed perspective will help you to drive forward in pursuit of your goals. Go ahead; I know you can do it.

Take Risks

What other characteristics do our mail counterparts have that we do not have? They are not adverse to taking risks. Successful women also have this characteristic. I recently talked to two female executives, Arlene and Kim. They launched their own business nine years ago. Our company just bought their business. It was well run, well designed, and is doing great. It was a great way for our company to get a head start into a new business line. If you were to ask these ladies their secret to success, it would be that they took calculated risks.

They bought the best information technology, and put in infrastructure for the larger company they wanted to be 'when they grew up'. Their risks paid off. The calculated risks that you take have a great potential to pay off.

Key Point: Success Entails Taking Calculated Risks.

Calculated risks that you take have a great potential to pay off.

We tend to err on the side of complacency. We accept things the way they are, we don't like to take risks. It is easier for us to accept the status quo. We accept the status quo, and by doing that, we are stepping aside for someone else to reap the rewards of well-taken risks. If we can risk our entire future on marrying a man, promising to love and to cherish for this day forward, surely we can take a calculated business risk. This risk will not be 'til death do you part.'

I'm sure you have heard, "nothing ventured, nothing gained." This has proven true for me in my career life. There are small risks, and there are big risks. It is a bit of a risk every time you take a new position or change jobs. There is a small risk when you blind copy your bosses' boss on an assignment due or emails directed at your boss. They are calculated risks. Even more so, there are risks in customer meetings, business decisions, and in day to day activities at work. Do you take risks?

We don't like to gamble, for the most part. Risks infer that we could potentially lose. Risks involve a potential sacrifice that many are not willing to take. Success entails taking calculated risks.

Admit When You are Wrong

This little tidbit of knowledge seems illogical to some of the women that I have mentored. Making mistakes is part of pressing the limits and doing the job you are being paid to do. You will make mistakes. It should be expected. The best way to over come these is to admit your mistakes, and move forward. I highly recommend showing your humanness. If you find that you were biting in your comments in a meeting, then apologize. If you misjudged someone, take them to lunch and ask them to forgive you. Openly admit your errors. You will find that this will gain the respect of the team of people that you work with. They will also be easier on you when you do lose your cool or make a mistake. They will be more apt to support you.

Key Point: Openly Admit Your Errors.

By admitting your mistakes, you will gain the respect of the team and they will be more apt to support you.

If you make a bad business decision, quickly admit your error and move in the correct direction. Bill Gates is on record saying that he will never do business over the internet. People make mistakes. The bigger mistake is not admitting your error and running in the correct direction as soon as you realize that you've made the error.

Chapter 6 "Attitude is Everything" Summary of Key Points:

- **Trust your own judgment; don't believe what you hear**
- **Hire smart people to replace you at some point**
- **Show appreciation to others**
- **Appreciation is a big motivator**
- **Search out the diamonds in the rough**
- **Create a new reality and a changed perspective for yourself**
- **Success entails taking calculated risks**
- **Openly admit your errors**

Chapter Seven

7. Taking on More Responsibility the Right Way

It is important to provide value to the company, as referenced in Chapter 3 on the three pillars of value. It is also important to take on additional responsibilities when asked. The repeated error that I made in my career was continually taking on additional responsibilities without valuing those in pay or bonuses. I ended up providing more and more value without an associated compensation. Have you ever tried to charge for something that you have been giving away? It is a difficult proposition. You probably received this advice from your mother very early in life.

Our male counterparts have done an excellent job of understanding their responsibilities and the value that they provide. In their area of responsibilities, they work to excel at it. When they achieve they receive more responsibility. When they are offered more responsibility, they make a demand/request for additional pay. If they are denied the additional pay, they usual still take on the responsibility with a future date to evaluate results and compensate accordingly. The additional responsibility is then expected to eventually result in additional pay/benefits/reward or a promised future promotion.

Key Point: When Offered More Responsibility, Request More Pay.

Bethany Williams

If you are denied the additional pay, still take on the responsibility with a future date to evaluate results and compensate accordingly.

Women I have talked to, including myself, tend to want to fix things and take on additional responsibilities. We take on things outside of our area that we haven't been given or we take on whatever we are given, out of a dire desire to do all that we can. Often it detracts from our given responsibilities. We shine less in our given area. Mentally, we need to associate additional responsibilities with compensation. If we were to buy a new house, and ask for special tile, we would not be surprised if that tile added additional cost to the deal. If you have moved from managing one department to five departments, shouldn't that account for additional pay or benefits? Trying to be recognized and paid for additional responsibilities AFTER THE FACT is very hard. Once you take on the additional four departments, you've allocated your existing pay to account for all five departments. You could look at this in two ways. One way is that you will not likely be downsized (surely they will not be able to find a man that would do that job for the pay you are probably accepting), or you could look at it as a lesson learned and remember Bethany's principal that says, *You Can't Charge for It After You Give it Away.*

Many women that I've mentored think about the risk. They are 'what if' kind of ladies. What if I am no longer able to fly "under the radar"? What if this amount of raise puts me in a vulnerable spot to then be canned? Remember the section on risk? The fact is, our male counterparts will not lose sleep wondering if making additional money will be the end of their career. They strive to make more money. This is why our male counterparts DO make more money.

In Chapter 8 on raises, we will discuss researching your value. You will then know your market worth. You have begun concentrating your efforts on the goals of the organization, as covered in Chapter 3. You are now being asked to take on additional responsibility. It should be a decision that you now move to a discussion of reward for the additional responsibilities that you are taking on.

Funny, we work with doctor's offices all the time in my job. The front desk staff NEVER want to ask for the co-payments that are due. We work with them to role play and work on requesting co-payments from patients. Maybe you could role play with a significant other in your house.

It might sound something like this:
Boss: I am looking to your leadership to help lead the X effort. There will be 3 additional FTEs reporting to you. I know that you will excel.
You: Wow, I am thrilled that you have the confidence in me to extend my current responsibilities. When will this transition take place?
Boss: June 1st.
You: Are there transitional next steps that you need me to follow through on? Administrative details, meeting with current supervisor, etc?
Boss: I will get you your action items by Friday.
You: Is there a title change?
Boss: No, one is not anticipated.
You: I would expect additional compensation to take on additional responsibilities.

Your role play will happen from this point of the conversation forward. He/she will have several varied responses, all of which will deny additional pay. Do you remember the minimalist approach? They will be trying to get you to do the maximum amount of work for the minimum amount of pay that they can offer.

Boss possible answer 1: There just isn't anything in the budget that I can offer you.
Boss possible answer 2: It is not the right time of the year, you know evaluations happen in X month.
Boss possible answer 3: We will wait and see how it goes.
Boss possible answer 4: That just isn't possible.

Options to Increase Your Value

You are working to increase your value. You can do this in a number of ways. In all the possible answers, you could:

1. **Ask for a title change.** At least if you have a higher title, you would get additional money if you left the organization and went to another company. Also, it may give you additional bargaining power when it is 'that time of the year for evaluations'.

2. **Ask for an official 'promotion.'** Companies can usually change your title, by adding a Sr. or something like that to your title, or they can 'promote you'. Oftentimes a promotion will give you (depending on policy for the company) a percentage bump in pay like 5% or 10% for example.

3. **Ask for a 're-evaluation' commitment at evaluation time.** You could request that your pay be considered for a larger than normal raise at the time of your next evaluation. You probably should

get an email on this one (what if he gets canned before your evaluation).

Don't feel bad if you get absolutely NOTHING out of the communication. You did make a statement. You set an expectation with your boss that additional responsibilities = additional pay/benefits. You set your worth and stated your position. This is valuable in the long run. Don't feel bad about asking for something and getting a 'no'. Also, you can't walk away thinking that you will never try that again. I know; we hate rejection. We hate to hear the word 'no' in any way, shape, or form. Next time he/she makes a request, they will be prepared that you are going to ask for additional pay. Next time they may say, 'yes'. The key is to not be discouraged by your inability to obtain results. You will have to practice at this. It will not go your way every time. Remember, they are trying to avoid paying you more. It is not going to be easy.

Key Point: Consider Other Options to Increase Your Value.

Ask for a title change, a promotion, or a designated future date to re-evaluate your value.

Women through time have ridden in covered wagons, given birth in obscure locations without medical treatment, battled for the right to vote and work, and battled through numerous other difficult tasks. Surely, you can begin to recognize your contributions to your companies and ask for additional pay when you receive additional responsibilities.

Not Accepting Responsibilities is Not an Option

You notice that I didn't mention not accepting the additional responsibility as an option. Yes, you could deny the additional responsibility, but it is not good for your brand or your image, or your career path. If you are truly working to get promoted, it is not usually a wise thing to do unless you have personal life issues that prevent you from doing it. If you are one of the women that are OK where you are, and you want to 'fly under the radar', than surely you can request that they find someone else with which to give this additional responsibility. Knowing what you want and where you want to end up is the key to knowing the right answer in this situation for you. Life entails choices.

If you do accept the additional responsibilities, you are back to the research. You will have to research your 'new' worth. Your previous research is outdated now unless the new responsibilities were inconsequential. I missed this step several times in my career.

Key Point: It is Not Good for Your Brand or Image to Turn Down Additional Responsibilities.

If you are truly working to climb the corporate ladder, accept responsibilities when given. It will shine a positive light on your image and your brand.

Can you believe at one point in my career I actually went from approximately fifteen direct reports to over 150 direct reports without getting any additional pay? In retrospect, it seems obvious that I should have requested a raise. But, I am imagining that you have a few of these 'obvious' times in your life that are running through your mind right now.

Well, like me, you cannot change the past. You can commit to changing the future. You can commit to react differently next time that you are faced with this situation.

Chapter 7 "Taking on More Responsibility the Right Way" Summary of Key Points:

- **When you are offered more responsibility, request more pay**
- **Consider other options to increase your value**
- **It is not good for your brand or image to turn down additional responsibilities**

Chapter Eight

8. What? Me, Ask for a Raise? How Could I?

Dealing with your Inability to Ask for Money

Let's face it: the statistics are not good. Did you know that less than four percent of women in America make more than $70,000/year? And, EVERY survey I've ever read says that women doing EXACTLY the same jobs as men earn nineteen to forty percent LESS, depending on the market. Did you get that? We are accepting from nineteen to forty percent LESS! Does that shock you? IT SHOULD SHOCK YOU. It should anger you. It should cause you to think about it. There are probably a hundred reasons that women don't choose to ask for raises, and only one thing that you should consider, the worst thing that can happen is they can say 'no.' And, more than that, THEY CAN'T say 'YES' if you don't ask.

We don't like to ask for what we want. We don't like to ask for what we need. This causes many problems in our relationships as well as problems at the office. I laughed once, sitting in on a relationship class, where she advised the women to ask for what they need. She advised that men do this, naturally. We as women often tend to try to manipulate the end result without a direct request. So, for instance, a man will ask for a back massage if he wants you to massage his back. A woman, on the other hand, may lean over and begin giving the man a back massage if she wants one. She is hoping that he will then want to turn and give her a massage. She is trying to use influence and manipulation to get what she truly wants. Men are more apt to be direct, "my back, your hands, now." This lifetime of us not being direct, is hurting us at the office and more importantly, in the pocketbook.

What would you do if you were about to sell your car? You would research to see how much it was worth. You would think about the condition of the car. The combination of these two things would drive your price. You would never think of telling someone, "pay me whatever you think is the right value for the car." Then, *why would you do that with your salary?* You need to react the exact same way you would as if you were selling a car.

First, you need to research your value. Many web sites, like www.Salary.com can give you ideas for expected salary amounts by job title for specific regions as well as company sizes. It will give you an idea of what you should be making. Then you need to evaluate your own educational background and credentials. If you are, for example, a coding expert, RHIA, MBA, Technician, etc, then that should figure into your value. If your value falls short of what you'd like it to be, take note of missing classes or credentials that could help. This will factor into your planning process for the future.

Key Point: Researching Your Value is an Important Step to Increase Your Pay.

Research your value, and determine your market worth.

Unfortunately, there is a distinct disadvantage to staying with a company for long periods of time. Once in the system, most companies have limits to the raises that they will give you, regardless of the responsibilities you take on or the promotions you receive. This is why an exit plan is so important. We will address that later on in this chapter and how to strategically move both your career and your salary forward.

What they may not tell you is that there are options other than straight pay increases. All of which you should consider asking for depending on how your negotiations are going.

A. **Stock Options**- These are options to purchase company stock at a set rate. If you, for instance, received a stock grant of 500 options at a current stock rate of $15 a share, they wouldn't be worth anything at the time of granting. They will only be worth something if the company does well enough that the stock goes up. You are betting on the success of the company. This enables the company to reward you if you are a major contributor without a direct cash outlay. Some of these benefits have eroded with requirement for the companies to recognize the award immediately as a hit to their bottom line. If you sell your options when the stock was at $20 a share, then you pay the $15 a share back to the company, and you keep $5 a share, or $5 X 500 = $2500.

The strike price is important. Oftentimes these are intended to keep you at the company, so they 'vest' over a period of years. You may be only able to sell 100 of the 500 options in the first year, and they may vest over a five-year period.

If they award you a very high strike price, then they are not doing you any favors. For example, if the current stock is trading at $15 a share, and they offer a strike price of $30 a share, don't consider this much of an asset.

These are more available at small to mid size companies, certainly much more difficult in large cap companies. Investigate to figure out your company's stance on options.

B. **Performance Bonuses**- Often you can negotiate for a performance bonus based on a goal in your area. These pre-defined cash bonuses can motivate you as well as help the company meet a major goal as well.

C. **Additional Vacation Days**- Always a good option if all else fails is to ask for additional time off. Even a boss with no power can oftentimes grant you additional paid time off.

D. **Flex Scheduling or Job Shares**- You could consider working a flex schedule, like four, ten hours days or propose a job share where two people work one position.

E. **Work at Home**- Option to work at home full- or part-time.

Companies have a set spending limit. They have a budget. That budget has to accomplish all the stated goals and achievements for that company. Similar to your own checkbook, they often run short on what they would really like to spend and accomplish. Okay, don't go getting sappy on me now and feel sorry for your company. The truth is, they will only pay WHAT THEY MUST to get by. Most companies take a minimalist approach. The minimum amount that they can pay you to keep you is the amount they will offer. They can only afford to pay raises to the top ten percent in the company. The faster they offer you a raise, the more underpaid you must be. They will tell you that they have nothing in the budget to give you. I have heard this many times, each time I received a substantial raise (after MUCH deliberation). So, needless to say, they really could give me a raise, but were just trying not to. If you are truly valuable, they can definitely find you additional pay.

Key Point: Companies Have a Set Spending Limit; Only the Top 10% of the Performers Will Receive Raises.

Your company has a budget that it must stay within. If you are TRULY valuable, they can DEFINITELY find you additional pay.

My first experience with this was five years into my employment. Having stayed at a technology company longer than people generally stay, I was underpaid. Not only that, but my research showed that I had contributed significantly to the bottom line. One example was an email from a major customer that indicated that their multi-million dollar deal would not have signed without my influence. I had many such examples that I had saved. I will address your success folder and ability to tout your successes in Chapter 13. This was my first experience with learning this. My current boss had taken the credit for my success, and although my department was slated for bonuses, I hadn't received any.

My first step was doing the research. I had to determine if my belief that I was underpaid could be substantiated. I had to determine my worth outside of the company, to then be able to determine my worth within the company. I polished up my resume and began interviewing for positions at other companies. At the time, it was the only way I knew that I could discuss salaries and to accurately determine my market worth. Today, with internet searching tools and salary surveys that you can purchase, there are many options. Not only did I discover that I was being vastly underpaid, but I received a job offer from the competition. It included a $5,000 sign on bonus, as well as a $15,000 annual bonus. The base salary was $15,000 more than I was currently making. It also included 1,500 stock options per year. This brought my new offer to:

$15,000 increase in base pay
$15,000 annual bonus
$ 5,000 sign on bonus
_____

$35,000 more CASH in the first year with a hefty dose of stock options.

I had already had the discussion with my boss that I was not satisfied with my pay and I had requested a pay raise, which was denied. As they said it, they had "no money in the budget." I prepared my letter of resignation and handed it in. I was amazed that they were somehow able to find the money in their budget. Isn't that surprising?

Do you remember what I said about the minimalist approach? If you are truly valuable AND you have built your brand and are recognized for your contributions, your company will most likely not want to let you go even after you find a better offer.

Bethany Williams

Key Point: Don't Be Afraid to Ask for What You Are Worth!

Once you have done your research and know your worth, don't be afraid to ask for what you are worth. Propose to your boss that you receive a raise.

I hadn't wanted to leave the company. I loved my job. I loved the people I worked with. But in order to protect my financial security and to ensure that I was being paid for my contributions, I had to prepare (and be ready to use) an exit plan.

The same company that advised me that there was no money in the budget for an increase was able to pony up the money when push came to shove. So, I'm telling you to BE ASSERTIVE. I'm telling you to STAND UP FOR YOURSELF. Your male counterparts are and they are BRINGING HOME nineteen to forty percent MORE THAN YOU ARE! There is a limited amount of money to go around, and they are being more straightforward, more demanding, and more determined.

I did once have a boss that truly took care of me, ensuring that I was being compensated accordingly. If you have a boss like this, you are very blessed. He gave me raises and bonuses even before I asked. He recognized my contributions and made sure to pay me market value. Unfortunately for me, he was soon promoted out of the department, and I lost the best boss I ever had. I still reported up to him, once removed. My job was much harder after knowing what it was like to have a great boss.

When was the last time you negotiated such a great deal for yourself, sufficient stock options, an incredible raise, etc., as to enable you to retire young, or retire in the event of a buyout? I know, I know—but, we all should be thinking that we can instead of thinking that it is impossible.

Winning Strategies Advice in Action: Asking for a Raise

"Bethany,
I need some advice. I have an interview tomorrow for a Laboratory Director position that I am hoping I will get. I have been working with the Medical Director for the past six years at my current position. Here's the question:
I have been with my company for six years….and I love it. I am currently working on a project for a new company within the system and I love it! For this project, I've received no extra pay, it has been strictly volunteer. There will be leadership positions available for the new hospital starting soon. If I leave my current position to work for this affiliated physicians group I will lose all my seniority where I am. If I were to come back in a year (if they hired me for the leadership position) I would start at the beginning again. Right now, I am 100% vested in my 401k, get five weeks of vacation, etc. But, if I get this other position it should be a significant increase in pay.
I guess if I am increasing my pay and my responsibility, I can't really go wrong—right?"
A. R., Ft. Worth, Texas

"Ah, the topic of pay, raises, and asking for additional monies. These are great questions and ones that we encounter all the time. There is no one answer. Figure out what is important to you. Everyone has different drivers that they consider important to them. If pay and promotion are high on your list, you will need to be willing to leave your current position to get it. You could advise your boss of your dilemma, advising that you really want to stay, but they could 'send you on your way.'

Determine what your work goals are. Write them out. Focus on where you want to go in your career, and the financial goals that you have. Make your opportunity decisions accordingly. You may choose at certain points in your life to sacrifice salary for a company you really like to work for or a boss/team that you really enjoy or work experience that is helping you build your resume.
Good luck." ~ Bethany

Requesting a Raise the Right Way

Once the research is done, you will need to be able to ask for a raise the right way. Pay, and raises, are about your contribution to the company. If you are contributing to the company's success, you should be paid your market value. <u>No one will track your successes</u> except for you. You are responsible to track your value. You cannot ask for a raise based on what someone else is making.

Your pay is based on your contribution, as well as pay grades for your type of position and geographic area. In a later chapter of the book, I will cover your success folder.

Winning Strategies for Women

This will help you annually as you request your raises.

Key Point: No One Will Track Your Successes (Except You).

You are responsible to track your value. Your pay is based on your contribution.

You don't 'ask' for a raise; you propose that you get a raise based on evidence of your contributions. I'm suggesting you be assertive. You don't want it to come off with a question at the end of the sentence. I have done X, Y, and Z in the last year, contributing significantly to the company's success. Tout all contributions. "I feel that my position is undervalued in this market space." Cite salary surveys and data from research. I am requesting that I be brought up to market value, which equates to a $X or $Y raise.

Key Point: Propose a Raise Based on Evidence of Your Contributions.

Cite salary surveys and market data. Request a specific amount with request for an answer by a specified date.

It is a little bit like asking your mom for spending money when you were a kid. Ask for more than you really want. If you want a $4,000 raise, ask for $6,000. They most likely won't give you what you ask for. If you want $2 more an hour, ask for $3 more an hour. Remember the minimalist approach. This will be their guiding principal.

Your Exit Plan

Your network is your most important asset. What if your employer says no to your proposals? You will need to research and explore an exit plan. Without an exit plan, you are at the mercy of whatever your employer wants to pay you and whatever position they want to put you in. Remember, your employer is motivated to pay you the least amount possible. You simply must accept whatever they dish out if you have not explored your other options. If you have no plan, than you are forced to whittle away accepting whatever they choose to pay you and living with whatever assignments come your way. Your male counterparts would not do that. They wouldn't accept that. This is why they get what they want. They wouldn't stay with the company under those circumstances. EVERY time I researched and prepared to exercise an exit plan, I fully intended on using it. I didn't want to. I wanted to stay. But, I do work for financial stability, and I owed it to my family and myself to make the most that I can make and so do you. You owe it to yourself and those that depend on you. So now you're asking, "how do I create an exit plan?"

Key Point: Always Have an Exit Strategy!

You have to have an exit strategy. You can achieve this in four easy steps.

1. **Take the Time to Research your Exit Plan**
2. **Consider Your Options**
3. **Go Window Shopping**
4. **Use the Ammunition**

Step 1: Take the Time and Effort to Research an Exit Plan

You have to be prepared to exercise an exit plan. The beginning step is to take the time and effort to research an exit plan. The internet makes this much easier than ever before. You have probably used the Monster employment web site (www.monster.com). This site allows you to post your resume, search for open jobs and apply online. It will give you an idea of the number of open positions in your area by title. A little research around the site will raise your awareness of the job market. If you are already in the over $100,000 salary range (lucky you), then The Marketing Ladder website (http://marketing.theladders.com) lists jobs that pay over 100K. There are numerous others, but these are the two that I've found to be the most valuable.

Step 2: Consider Your Options

The next step is to consider your options. What would you do if you were laid off tomorrow? What steps would you take? Are there contacts that you know in the industry that you would immediately call? Call them, tell them that you want to keep your eyes on the horizon, that you are not actively looking for a position but are curious as to what is out there. Let them know that if they have any ideas, you'd love to discuss them. You should stay in contact with these sources regardless of your current situation. Have you been staying at home for a few years? It doesn't matter, you still need to be having coffee occasionally with people you know in the industry. You never know what life will send your way. Be prepared for the unexpected, and then, when surprises hit, they won't be unexpected. You could be caught without warning at some point in your career. Many people have been in this difficult market. Considering your options ahead of time ensures that you are prepared, and ready if anything does occur. It also makes you a much better negotiator. Knowing your 'out' option will help you to fight harder for your worth.

Step 3: Go Window Shopping

The third step is to window shop. You've done it before, surely you know how. Surely you have gone to the mall and tried on a pair of shoes to see how they feel. I'm requesting that you interview, send out a few resumes, and put your feelers out. Don't refuse to do this just because you've heard it is a 'tough market' out there. Work on getting an offer of employment. Start with your contacts in the field. If you don't have contacts in the field, make some. Strategically invite someone to coffee or lunch that you met at a recent educational event. If you aren't attending any educational events in your career path, than GO-LEARN- MEET. At least twice a year participate in educational seminars or events.

I know what you are thinking: *But Bethany - I don't want to leave my present employer. I like it here. I have learned the ropes and would like to stay right where I am.* I 'm not asking you to purchase the shoes or take them home. I'm asking you to window shop. It is a mandatory step in getting a raise and ensuring that you always have a job. If you aren't interested in promotions, pay increases, or achievement at the office, or worried about job loss, then you don't have to worry about this. I know you are. Read on.

Step 4: Use the Ammunition

The next step is to use the ammunition that you have gathered. Remember, your employer is going to tell you that they cannot afford to give you a raise. They will probably tell you that they don't have the money in the budget. There are hundreds of excuses that they will use. Each of these possible excuses may or may not actually be true. *The truth is, they can only afford to give the highest raises to the ones that they will lose or their top performers.* Employees that plan to stay, are not targets for large, if any, pay increases in many companies. You may go into your boss's office, and request more pay. He/she will either tell you they will get back to you, or say 'no', not in the budget, sorry. You will say, "That isn't acceptable. I have accomplished X, Y, Z for the company, and have researched my value. Current positions in this area, for my job title are paying X dollars above my current salary."

This is your second swing. The "I have researched the market" swing. The third swing will preparing to use your exit card. You will want to take careful consideration before using this Ace in the Hole. You have to be prepared to leave and take the other offer if you play this card. They may just say, "Okay, thank you for working here." It is a risk, one that you will have to weigh carefully before you use it.

If they truly value you and you have provided value to them, they will offer you more money that may or may not accompany a change in title and other benefits. Remember, you ONLY get what you ask for. You might be thinking, "I've never gotten stock options." Well, have you ever asked for them? Make a list in advance of your requests. At one point in my career about three years into my employment, I went to my boss with the following demands:

Demands
1. **Option to work at home one day a week**
2. **Title change**
3. **Minimal additional bonus per deal closing**

Remember, I was new at this and I was, admittedly, not very good at it. I wish I had some solid instruction or a good mentor coaching me early in my career. It would have moved me forward much faster. It is *the* reason that I assist you today with your requests from around the globe about pay dilemmas.

Well, at the time, I had no exit plan. So my demand sounded something like this, "I have accomplished X, Y, and Z at this company: with major contributions to the bottom line. I am requesting 1, 2 and 3 in order to bring me to market value and high satisfaction with my position."

My boss denied all three demands. It was funny, actually, in retrospect. What was I going to do if he said no? Was I going to threaten to hit him with a wet noodle? Once my requests were denied, I began to research an exit plan. Like a typical woman, it took me getting angry to look at my options. Our male counterparts don't need to be ticked off to get to this point. They instinctively search for the better offers, investigate their pay options, and move themselves into better positioning.

After looking around for a month, I received a job offer from another department in the company. I took that position and received the following:

- $20,000 more a year on my base pay
- New Job Title
- Work at home approved

I was actually better off than if I have received an approval for my demands. I was making more money than I had even requested. Always take life by the horns. If you don't get what you want, figure out another way to tackle the beast that is your job. You are not a victim; you are the driver of your life at work. You are driving the bus that is your career, your career journey, and your wages.

Constantly re-evaluate where you are, what you are doing, and where you are going on a six-month rotating basis. This will help you in planning your career path and career steps.

Keeping Your Eye on the Horizon, Avoiding Future Job Loss and Planning Your Future

Most of the women that I have mentored, are not really concerned about job loss until they are staring it in the face. Being aware of what is coming down the road is something that we should keep constant vigilance over. We need to keep an eye on the horizon. One of my direct reports when I was in Product Strategy was responsible for HIPAA, the Health Insurance Portability Act. This very invasive security regulation rocked the industry for several years and still has reverberations in the industry today. Many companies added positions to cope with the impending HIPAA regulations. Sara was hired to facilitate our company through the HIPAA shock wave.

After we weathered the HIPAA storm together, we soon after began to plan for Sara's future. We recognized that companies wouldn't continue to fund these positions. We sat down and put together a plan to move Sara over time into other responsibilities to replace her HIPAA responsibilities. We wanted to make sure that she was continually able to contribute to the company as well as building a skill-set that she could use after the HIPAA storm.

She begin to take on Product Strategy for the Registration, Access, and EDI components of the product. These valuable skillsets would help ensure that she had a job either at our company or another company for her future. Using an eye on the horizon, we were able to build a plan for her future to ensure that she had a job.

It is important that we look down the road and anticipate upcoming events. Some are easy to see coming, others are more difficult to see. Our goal is to see danger coming down the road in advance. We want to prepare for upcoming events before they happen. Do you think your department will be outsourced in a year or so? Have you thought about what you would do in that situation? While you have a job is a great time to think about your exit plan. Remember, you need to always have an exit plan. Always be ready to act upon it. Remember Chapter Four? An exit plan is your last ditch effort when you can't work things out with your current employer OR when something unforeseen happens. Keeping an eye on the horizon, however, is a mandatory pre-cursor to job success. The 'it will never happen to me' downsizing thinking will not work. You need to plan for the inevitable. It could happen. It could happen to you. If it did, what would you do? Begin to plan for it today.

Planning Your Future

Your planning job wasn't over when you announced your major in college or decided what to do 'when you grew up'. Planning for your future is a constant part of your responsibilities going forward. Plan out the progression you would like to take in your career. Do you have a goal of a particular job that you would like to end up in? Having a career path pre-figured out can help you make career choices as you go throughout life. It doesn't always work out the way you have planned, I recognize that. But having a plan is a precursor to success. You should be able to make updates to this plan annually when you do your annual reviews. Chapter 13 will talk about these reviews in detail.

The path you choose and where you want to end up will help you when you receive job offers. When I was early on in my career, working as a Financial Counselor at a hospital, I came to a fork in the road. I was being offered a job in Administration as an Executive Assistant to the CEO. The pay would have been more than I was currently making. I decided that being an Executive Assistant to the CEO was not the career path that I wanted to be on. I wanted to **be CEO** someday, and I thought that my career path would be better off with a move to a middle management position, working on a team with the CEO, than working as an executive assistant to the CEO.   Your career goals will help you make decisions necessary to further your career. Choose jobs that put you in the path towards the positions that you want.

Chapter 8 "What? Me, Ask for a Raise?" Summary of Key Points:

- **Researching your value is an important first step to increasing your pay**
- **Companies have a set spending limit. Only the top 10% of performers receive raises**
- **Don't be afraid to ask for what you are worth**
- **No one will track your successes (except you)**
- **Propose a raise based on evidence of your contributions**
- **Always have an exit strategy**

Chapter Nine

9. Getting Everyone in the Company to Work for You (or so it seems...)

For most of the things that you need to accomplish, you will need others' assistance. Really, nothing seems to come through without a team approach. But how do you really gain the acceptance and help from the team, when members are on other teams reporting up through other managers? Determining how to do this is a crucial ring on the ladder to your success. You are but a small piece of the puzzle that will create solutions for your company. You must depend on numerous other casts of characters that are your co-workers. Each of you seem to have varying objectives on the surface, with no common goals in sight. In order to succeed in true teamwork, you will need to find those common goals. You will learn to spend more of your time working on projects that you can get others to assist in with group goals. Truly I have found that Together Everyone Achieves More (T.E.A.M.). The most successful people you will ever meet have discovered that success comes from teamwork. It is about the company achieving its goals, not just you meeting your objectives.

Key Point: Success Comes from Teamwork.

The most successful people you will ever meet have discovered that success comes from teamwork.

Incentives

It didn't take me long to realize that employees are GREATLY motivated by incentives, no matter what level they are within the company. If you are struggling with getting cooperation with a project at work, I'm betting that his/her incentives are discouraging his/her participation. Most everyone has a list of goals to achieve this year. The higher up the ladder you go, the more incented you are to achieve those goals. At some level and above, they generally are tied to large bonuses and, in most cases, at the highest levels not meeting your goals could mean losing your job.

I once felt like I was running down a hill backwards on a project that I was trying to get participation on. It was frustrating to feel that a key senior leader in another business unit didn't seem aligned. Every day was a struggle. It was a project given to me by the CEO. I figured that the noncompliance I was feeling was due to misaligned incentives. I requested that the senior leader's incentives be changed to align with the stated goals. We experienced a night and day difference at work. The senior leader that was causing so many problems began moving the project forward and almost steam rolled over me to make sure that it got done. The difference was astounding.

I began to evaluate the incentives of other leaders in the organization. Knowing that the Implementation's VP, for example, had an incentive based on billable hours as one facet of the evaluation was very valuable. I then knew that if I needed help from his organization, I needed to figure out a way to get the customer to allow some 'billable hours.' I had been going about this the wrong way. Each person that I needed participation from needed to 'want' to help at the core of their incentives in order to get the spring forward, jump on it kind of reaction that I was hoping for.

If my project had no incentive for the other group, I lowered it on my priority list to work since I really didn't have allotted time for projects that would not go anywhere. We had much to accomplish and I had to take on the pieces that were most likely to move.

This took creative thinking to evaluate the things that my team needed to accomplish, determine the necessary team, and consider their plausibility for their wanting to participate. I then worked with my direct reports to determine our strategy for requesting the help we needed and for accomplishing the projects.

In a matter of 18-24 months, my team became known as the "Team that can get things done." We were recognized across the company for our ability to accomplish tasks that others could not accomplish. We used, of course, all of the ideas in this book, but knowing the incentives of the parties was a critical piece of the puzzle. You can use this same technique.

◆ ◆ ◆ ◆ ◆ ◆

Key Point: Evaluate the Incentives for Others that You Work With.

Move projects to the top of your list based on their ability to align with the incentives of others in the organization. If you can find aligned incentives, you are more probable to achieve the task or assignment.

◆ ◆ ◆ ◆ ◆ ◆

Once we understood what the other leaders both needed and wanted to accomplish, we were able to provide a win/win. We could show them how our projects would aid them in their goals, and as a result- we excelled in our accomplishments. We proposed internal projects that provided a win/win solution set. This ability to plan for success made our team the most accomplished team in the company.

Knowing Their Hearts' Desires

Sometimes it pays off to know what really motivates people even above their success at the office. Most people have something that they are passionate about. A skillset or area that they LOVE to do. For some positions in the company, this may be something that they don't get to exercise while at work. Our Vice President of Sales' Administrative Assistant in Chicago loved to travel and help out with administrative duties for focus group meetings. She didn't get the chance to do this very often. She shared this information with me when I was at the Chicago office once. I made note of this.

Key Point: Find Passion Lying in Wait.

Keep your eyes and ears open. Discover what employees around you really like to do. You can then use that knowledge to suggest them for projects that use their skill set.

113

The next time my group had a focus group that we needed to plan for St Louis, I called the VP of Sales in Chicago to see if I could 'borrow' his administrative assistant. He was on vacation or not working the week we needed her, if I remember correctly, so he said 'sure'. She flew to St Louis and handled all of the administrative tasks. She was amazing. Our focus group went off handsomely. It was on a low budget, yes, but was well run, efficient and professional.

Keep your eyes and ears open. Discover what employees around you really like to do. You can then use that knowledge to suggest them for projects that use their skillset. You can become an employee advocate, of sorts. You may find that a project that you are working on needs that skillset. These employees will be dying to pitch in if you have truly found their strengths.

An administrative assistant in Dallas used to work for a VP who traveled often. I noticed as I walked by her desk that she was frequently bored with nothing to do. I asked her what she liked to do. She said that she was in school for graphic design. I was working on a product that had no brochures at the time, so she began to help me design brochures for the product line. We also worked together to redo all the PowerPoints and the reporting brochures. It has been ten years since we did this and the collateral pieces that we developed are still in use.

In this case, I was new to the company, so didn't ask permission to use the executive assistant. Today, I would ask if I could. She was incredibly gifted, and our company benefited from it. I recognized her contribution, and she was rewarded. She also got to do something that she liked to do, rather than sit in boredom every time the VP was on the road. Well, long gone are the days of one exec admin to one VP ratios, but I'm sure that there are still opportunities to find someone's 'heart's desires' and use their skills to move something forward that you are working on.

Expect Obstacles

It seems our whole lives we are told to "try to get along". We begin to formulate ideas that we must get along with everyone at work and that we should avoid obstacles. Just the opposite is true actually. If you are proposing a new idea that is different from anything your company has ever done, you will encounter obstacles. Avoiding those at all costs will only lead to inhibiting your own success. You are not pressing the limits if you don't encounter obstacles. When I took over the 'sunsetted' product line, there were obstacles everywhere. I, at times, thought about wearing amour to the office to enable me to live through the next month. I was targeted, treated badly, and badmouthed. It was such a joy. Laugh. My point is that what is RIGHT for the COMPANY MAY BE DIFFICULT for people in the company to accept.

Key Point: Expect Obstacles.

If you are proposing a new idea that is different from anything that your company has ever done, you will encounter obstacles.

If you know the goals and objectives of the company and you know that you are working to achieve those, everything else is noise.

Early on in our careers, we don't expect obstacles. Often, we never learn to truly anticipate them. I suffered from this in my career. Each time I encountered obstacles, I did so with shock and horror. Once I realized that obstacles were a sign that I was pressing the limits, trying new things, and opening up horizons, I begin to accept obstacles as a part of success.

I also encountered people that didn't want things to succeed, just because it might reflect on their leadership, since they were leading before me. March on and pay no attention to the flack around you. If you know the goals and objectives of the company and you know that you are working to achieve those, everything else is noise. I learned to work very hard to get along with people that I put in the category of 'people that can get things done.' I categorized everyone in two categories:

- ✓ People that can get things done
- ✓ People that do not get things done, for whatever reason

For people that fall into the second category, don't spend a lot of time worrying about what they think. If people are movers and shakers and are accomplishing goals and getting things done in the company, work diligently to get along with them.

Bethany Williams

When I was discouraged by obstacles that I encountered, I would read Walt Disney's story, or some other greatly inspirational tale of someone who did not give up.

My son, Brandon, came home from school the other day with one. He said that Edison once said that he had discovered two hundred ways not to invent electricity before he figured out all the elements necessary to make it work. Can you believe that all of these had to be working before electricity could happen?

- ✓ The parallel circuit
- ✓ A durable light bulb
- ✓ An improved dynamo
- ✓ The underground conductor network
- ✓ The devices for maintaining constant voltage
- ✓ Safety fuses and insulating materials, and
- ✓ Light sockets with on-off switches[1]

Can you imagine how many obstacles he ran into before he invented and refined all seven of these? Then he went on to discover a whole host of other things from telephones to movie making devices. Needless to say, he didn't let obstacles get in the way. Funny, actually, that I have been inspired by Edison for so long, and now that my company has been acquired, I am now working for Edison General Electric. Actually, they dropped Edison from the name years ago and now it is called General Electric.

---

[1] The Inventions of Thomas Edison_.
http://inventors.about.com/library/inventors/bledison.htm#Lightbulb

Random Positive Comments

Think random acts of kindness, only translate it to random positive comments. Getting others to work as if they were on your team requires positive affirmation. It will require that you positively recognize other's contribution verbally. You will do this out loud and often. I suggest you do this in front of others. It doesn't matter if the person you are speaking about is there or not. It will get back to them. Believe it or not, even positive information does travel, just not near as fast as negative information. It may take anywhere from a week to a month for a positive statement to float back to the person you were talking about. A negative comment makes its way back in less than 2 business days. So be wary, that one can come back to bite you.

◆ ◆ ◆ ◆ ◆ ◆

Key Point: Verbally Recognize Others.

If you can spot their strengths, bring those out in the conversation. Positively recognize other's contributions verbally.

It is not a good idea to cut others down, even in jest. Work to build others up and it will pay back in untold benefits. It will be important to touch base with people even when you don't need something from them. Only calling on someone when you need something will quickly move you to the bottom of their call back list. Call them simply to check on their last vacation, or how an account is going. Then when the time comes that you do need something, they will be more apt to take your call.

Make sure that you commend them for their contributions
and work on projects as it arises. If you can spot their
strengths, bring those out in the conversation.
Example: I knew that you would do well with X client,
you are a great communicator and have a special way with
accommodating difficult situations.

Sometimes, employees don't recognize their own strengths.
We had someone on our team that was frustrated with
leadership and really looking for a way off the team. Every
time I would run into him, I would comment on his
strengths. He was an amazing detail person. He could put
together detailed spread sheets of task oriented initiatives
and track them from a very high level down to the minutest
detail of data. He organized a Product Upgrade document
that was brilliantly done. He enjoyed being in the detail
and ensuring that others accomplished tasks that he could
then organize into a solution for the entire company. He
was great at what he did. His boss, however, didn't know
how to merge his skill set into the necessary tasks for the
team. He did find a position in the company to be content.
Always recognize the positive in everyone.

Chapter 9 "Getting Everyone in the Company to Work for You" Summary of Key Points:

- Success comes from teamwork
- Evaluate the incentives of others that you work with
- Find passion lying in wait
- Expect obstacles
- Verbally recognize others

Chapter Ten

10. Finding Value in Every Step

The most important key to climbing the ladder is to ensure that you are adding value to the company in every step. It is imperative that the value you add FAR exceed the salary you are being paid. It is like a proverbial checkbook, if the company starts out with $100,000 in a checkbook and pays you $50,000, and you are only benefiting the company $30,000 than you will run out of money in 'the checkbook' in a matter of time.

Transactions	100,000 balance
-50,000 pay	50,000
+30,000 benefit to the company	80,000
-50,000 pay	30,000
+30,000 benefit to the company	60,000
-50,000 pay	10,000
+30,000 benefit to the company	40,000
-50,000 pay	- 10,000

It doesn't take long to wipe out the balance if the benefit amount is less than you are being paid. I know what you are thinking, You want to tell me that it doesn't work that way. That there are some positions that are PURE cost and do not bring anything into the company. Well, I am advising you to find a way to benefit the company in a way that you can put a dollar amount on it. If you are a telephone operator for AT&T, than maybe you should volunteer for a six sigma, or other quality program on cost savings in your department. Figure out a way that you can point to a dollar amount and have contributed to either SAVING that money or BRINGING IN additional revenue to the company.

I find that many women that I talk to have 'detached' themselves from the thinking of their company as a business, and from them having anything to do with the balance, either positive or negative. It is this detached thinking that puts you at risk of being downsized or even worse, fired. It could even be worse than that. You could be stuck in a continuous job going no-where with minimal to no raises. You could be in a job that holds you back and causes you to live with the 'at least I can buy food' mentality. Our male counterparts would not LIVE with mediocrity. And they certainly wouldn't live with just enough money to buy food.

It will take a little time to begin a new awareness of the financial picture. Try to start thinking about expenses at work as if you were paying them yourself. You should be angry about a co-worker that fills out her time sheet that she was in for three days, when she only was there for two. It should frustrate you to see people standing around for WAY too long, wasting TOO MUCH time.

Key Point: Begin a New Awareness of the Financial Picture.

Start thinking about expenses at work as if you were paying them yourself.

In order to move to the next level, you need to begin to find value for your company in EVERYTHING that you do. Once you start thinking with more of an owner's perspective, you will be amazed at what you see that you didn't notice just the week before.

Re-shaping to Bring Enormous Benefit

Are there areas of your job that you could reform or transform to bring enormous benefit to the company? Do you control a process that has never worked right or work on a team that utilizes such a process? Have you ever wondered how much that process costs the organization? Well, I suggest you strive to figure it out, and then solve it or help to solve it.

Here I find that we don't want to admit that we have an area that is ill performing. Admit it! ANNOUNCE IT! And announce that it is going to get some major attention and brainstorming to discover how you can do it differently. Acknowledging a big problem in your area will not get you downsized. Ignoring that problem into infinity and NEVER recognizing it or solving it WILL GET YOU DOWNSIZED! So, don't be afraid of admitting a weakness. Be afraid of NOT admitting a weakness and letting it grow and turn into your archilles heel. Here, we are disadvantaged. Finding it tougher in the workforce as women, we feel that there is no room for failure. We simply cannot admit to our failures. Well, like it or not Ladies, we MUST. It is the only way to solve these and move forward. That is what our male counterparts would do. They would acknowledge, and attempt to solve. Ok, so yes, maybe the organization would be easier on them if they could not solve it. But, you must concentrate on the positive and you cannot avoid admitting mistakes or errors in your area just because you believe that you are better off not mentioning it. The company is not better off by you not mentioning it. Think like the owner, remember? It is not about how you look, it is about forwarding the companies initiatives and moving the company forward.

Key Point: Ignoring Problems that Exist will Get You Downsized.

Acknowledging a big problem will not get you downsized. Ignoring the problem into infinity and never recognizing it or solving it will get you downsized.

It is a bit like an alcoholic. If we do not admit the areas of weakness, than we will never attack them or solve them. If an alcoholic refuses to admit his/her problem, the problem will live on forever. Problems do not go away until we embrace them, acknowledge them, and decide to change them. It is the only way we move toward resolution.

What are the Highest Committed Goals of the Organization?

I bring this up one more time. What are the highest committed goals of the organization. You now have found these and taped them up on your desk, right? By this chapter of the book you should be weighing in your performance and benefit to the company against these committed goals. Are you directly impacting these goals?

Does your everyday work forward the company further in its initiatives?

This is the report card that you will weigh your performance against. Your daily activities and objectives will be weighed against the highest committed goals of the organization. It is at this point of the mentoring that often it breaks down. The women struggle with the concept of having to directly impact the highest goals of the organization. They see themselves as so far down on the totem pole as to never directly impact the highest committed goals of the organization. This is a dangerous place to be. It is really just a mindset change. Mentally, you have to accept that you indeed can contribute daily to these goals. You then need to think of yourself as an active player on the team. Without your contribution, the game would/could stall.

Key Point: Accept that You Can Contribute to the Highest Committed Goals of the Organization.

Think of yourself as an active player on the team. Without your contribution, the game would stall.

You have to believe in yourself and your ability to create change. It is an exercise in believing in yourself and getting yourself into a position to absolutely make change. You can either be a major contributor or not based on your ability to believe in yourself and your capabilities.

Actively denote your thinking and your time to achieving these goals.

It might surprise you to learn that you could be your biggest obstacle in your strive to the top of the company. Your inability to believe in yourself could keep you right where you are, without promotions or additions in your pay. I also learned this valuable lesson the hard way. I would see a promotion come up, and not apply for it. My own insecurities about maybe not being ready would keep me from applying for the job. Someone else would apply and I would train them. They would miserably fail, quit and the position would be open again. This time I would have worked up the confidence to apply and get the position. After a period of time I realized that I had wasted a year training the other guy and then watching him fail. If I had the confidence in myself a year earlier, I could have avoided all that work and difficulty.

If you have little faith in yourself, then go back to chapter one and start the book over. I want you to feign confidence until you build faith in yourself. It will come over time as you recognize little successes. You will notice that others sometimes believe in you before you do. Give yourself the benefit of the doubt. Trust in your abilities. Take the next move. Once you can do this, you will be ready to proceed to the next chapter.

Chapter 10 "Finding Value in Every Step" Summary of Key Points:

- Begin a new awareness of the financial picture
- Ignoring problems that exist will get you downsized
- Accept that you can contribute to the highest committed goals of the organization

Chapter Eleven

11. Touting Your Success from the Mountaintops

Your Success Folder

One piece of advice that I wish I had learned early on, is to document and record tidbits from your work history. You need to track your successes, as you will do a better job than anyone you ever report to.

Keep a folder of significant accomplishments as well as notes, cards or letters that you receive from staff or customers. I once received a $10,000 bonus out of an email that I had printed out and saved about a deal that I had contributed to. It was from a lead decision maker at a customer site that credited me with the deal. Well worth saving, wouldn't you say?

I made it a habit to request letters of recommendation from leaders while I was still employed, and not looking for work. These I added to my Success Folder. I also suggest keeping a printout of each job description in there as well. You are your own enterprise. You are responsible for advertising and tracking of you/yourself as a product. Think of yourself as a corporation. You own all rights and advertising permissions for yourself. If you create a good sellable brand for yourself, you will be paid handsomely. This thinking needs to begin early on in your career since decisions you make early will continue to follow you throughout your career. If you truly owned a product to sell, you would create a marketing plan for that product. You would envision where you wanted that product to go.

This is no different. Tracking your success is a key ingredient in this journey to the top.

Key Point: Keep a Folder of Your Successes.

Keep a folder of significant accomplishments as well as notes, cards or letters that you receive from staff or customers.

It is easier to build this folder slowly, otherwise you will put it off and never even start it. It will be a tool accessible to you when, and if , you ever have to look for work. The first step is to buy a folder that will be the container for your Success Folder. Then, annually when you do your annual review of your accomplishments, you will quickly review contents of this folder. AS things happen throughout the year, you will throw the printed emails and letters into the folder (to be organized at a later time). If you are ever caught without a job on short notice, you will have the beginnings for your tools to look for work.

This folder should make it easier for an employer assessing your skill-set and experience to see where you have been and what you have accomplished. Educational information/degrees and classes that you have taken should be included in this folder. It has enabled me over the years to get a job often times on first interviews, since the folder had all pertinent information. It makes you credible. It enables the prospective employer to 'validate' your resume without making phone calls or other tedious follow up tasks. It also makes you stand out in front of the pack. It will be your pressure for a 'close' at the end of the interview.

Leafing through the folder should give one a cursory review of what your resume says. If you have that you are licensed in a particular area, proof of that would be in the folder. Here is a quick and dirty check list of information for inclusion in your Success Folder.

Success Folder Contents

1. Resume
2. Job Descriptions from Current and Previous Jobs
3. Letters of Recommendations
4. Affirming emails from customers and employees
5. Certificates/Degrees
6. Pertinent Membership in National Organizations
7. Any articles you have written for trade publications

Communicating your Accomplishments through Memos and Emails

Your success folder is only one ingredient in your branding initiative. The next significant contribution to your brand is regular communication of accomplishments in your area. Think of it as your obligation to keep everyone in your circle of influence informed on current operations in your area. Announcements, updates, and other pertinent notifications should go out to notify others of information that might affect them. Women who have climbed the corporate ladder have become experts at this.

Did your team just accomplish a significant task? Even if you are not the leader of that team, an update email that is well written could go far. You must first determine the audience for such a message. We often forget this step in a successful career. Think of it like this. It does no good to be GREAT if no one knows that you are great. It is your responsibility to make sure that your team is recognized. That includes everyone you work with on your team and your supervisor. Remember, you are building a brand. This announcement/update should be brief, contain bulleted lists, and recognize all that contributed to the accomplishment.

To: Leadership Team, Deployment Team, Marketing Team

From: You

_____(company name) made significant strides forward today when _____(name of your team) completed the project to _____(x, y or z).

The goals of this initiative include:
- Improving customer response time
- Improving employee satisfaction
- Lowering cost to provide services
  (insert goals here)

This couldn't have been accomplished without the dedication and commitment of our team. Many thanks goes out to _____,_____,_____(list out the participants).

Please feel free to contact me with any questions. (Name) (Title) (phone number) (email address)

In building a brand, the more often you see/hear or notice the brand, the more success the brand has. As we apply this to you, as a brand, it is important that you are 'seen' often as are your successes. Anywhere from 6 to 10 of the 'successful completion of significant' tasks emails should go out directly from you annually. OK, part of you is thinking, do I really want to go through all of this? Well, how badly do you want to succeed? What if I told you that following this plan would lead you to a higher salary, absolutely. Companies PAY MORE for a 'brand' that they know what to expect from. As you build yourself up to be a performer, and to get things done (and they will know since you will be telling them), then you are surely to be promoted and to make significantly more money. My salary has increased by $100,000 in the last several years. YES, INCREASED by $100,000 a year. That would be worth your effort, wouldn't it?

Key Point: Regularly Advertise Your Success.

Send out six to ten emails or reports annually to communicate your successes.

Advertisers sit around thinking of 'different' ways to attract your attention as a consumer. They mail you different kinds of envelopes, and use all sorts of tactics to get your attention. Creativity can lend a hand in your pursuit of enhancing your brand. Email has become somewhat passé. It is losing its effectiveness. I have, on occasion, printed Memos and delivered them to the desktop or chair of senior leadership. They stood out because they were different than other communications. Once you become very familiar with leaders in organization, than anything goes. I once sent a message in chocolate. They never really know what to expect from me, other than consistent and regular communication. Not all of your communication will always be good, but another chapter will deal with communicating bad news.

The business unit I work in has over 2,500 employees, with offices around the globe. At a recent executive conference, the CEO told me that he receives regular emails from only four of those 2,500 employees (outside of his direct reports and direct associates). Remember, you are a building a brand. Don't be afraid to make your brand known. If you have something of significance to say, say it. Obviously, you will stand out. Less than one percent of the population of our business unit communicates directly with the CEO.

BIO

A biography is a great tool to record and document your career progress as you move up the ladder. A biography should give a work history for you. It tells the reader why you are 'worthy.' When you write your first one, you may not be. (Remember the chapter on believing in yourself?)

If you are worthy, and you haven't yet written one, shame on you. That is okay, though. You can write one now. I insist; before you move to the next page, write a quick and easy bio, whether or not you feel worthy.

Key Point: Create a Biography if You Don't Already Have One.

It is a great tool to record and document your career progress as you move up the ladder.

Your Biography:

BIOGRAPHY

_____(your name) is the
_____(title of your current job) at
_____(compa
ny you work for) working to
_____(standard
company goal or business statement of purpose).

Prior to her current role at
_____(company),
_____(last name) was
_____(what was your
title and what did you do?)

_____
_____.

_____(last name) received her
_____(name of degree) in
_____-(specialty)   from
_____(university) .

This is a good start. Congratulations. Now I suggest you write a Bio that reflects where you would like to be in five to seven years from now. Picture your Bio as you progress up the corporate ladder.

Annual Self Evaluations

Some companies require that you assess yourself every year, and some do not. Without an honest post year evaluation, you really don't give yourself enough direction to move forward in the coming year.

I suggest every year, that you write up a summary of your year. This suggestion comes at you whether or not your employer requires it. What were your accomplishments? It is worthwhile to put quite a bit of effort into the record of your successes and failures. If you have very little to write about, then resolve to change that in the next year. We file our taxes, probably because it is against the law if we don't. We fill out mandatory 'write ups' of our performance over the last year (in order to get that pilfry raise). Why don't you spend some time writing up (solely for yourself) what you did all year? You did do something this year, right? Did you contribute to a project that is propelling your company forward? If not, why not do that in the next year? This annual review is your chance to ask yourself if you really are set on making a difference at your place of employment. It is also your chance to decide that if you are not, you will start now.

Key Point: Write an Annual Summary of Your Accomplishments.

Whether or not your employer requires it, summarize your contributions to your employer for the year. Keep these summaries in your success folder.

So, you agree to do this. Some of you will find no problem writing down an evaluation of your performance this year. Others of you need more gentle prodding. You begin to write one. Then immediately you are staring down a blank sheet of paper. OK, I'll tell you the easiest way to do this if you fall into the latter category. You will begin by resolving to do it next year. OK, stay with me here, sounds a bit like procrastination, I know. Put 'YEARLY EVALUATION' on a manila folder. All throughout the year as small accomplishments happen, scribble a note and throw it into the folder. If it is an email or note from your boss, then you throw that in the folder. Then at the end of the year, you will have a great jumpstart on your paper.

If you take the first route, I will lay out for you content for this paper. Let's start with the Table of Contents.

I.   Year in Review
II.   Projects/major efforts/successes
III.   Customer/employee/supervisor feedback
IV.   Small successes
V.   Goals for the Upcoming Year
        a. Professional
        b. Personal
VI.   Career Goals/Plans for five years in the future

Keep a copy of this write up for your success folder. This annual record will profile your career. You will have this review even as you change jobs and/or locations. It will be continuity of where you have been and where you are going as your life changes. If you have a college degree, than I can picture that you have spent hours and hours writing term papers. If you don't, then that is just some pure fun waiting for you if you ever choose to tackle this great feat. Some term papers take weeks to write. We sweat over them, we fall asleep on them, we stay up all night to write them. A few months after that paper, we begin on another and that one is long faded from our memory. All the painstaking effort we put into it is short lived. I am asking that you spend that kind of effort documenting what you contributed in the past year. So what if you stay up all night ONE night to document that accomplishment. Five years from now, it will still be an important piece of your work history. It will not fade out of existence like all the effort that you poured into those term papers.

We really tend not to think through the long term effects of these little 'successful strategies.' I am not advising that you do this to ruin a weekend or take away your free time. I am encouraging you to spend time reviewing your work contributions for the last year. Each year, your papers will become more sophisticated and include more pertinent details of your success. You will begin to gain confidence just by your annual reminders to yourself of what you have accomplished. Annually, we review our tax information and file a statement with the IRS. This strategy advises to annually 'file' a contribution review.

Of course, these are not just for your reading pleasure. These documented success yearly reviews will accompany your annual review. Once a year you will forward this to your supervisor and possibly to his/her supervisor. Depending on where you would like to end up in the company, you may even forward it on to the CEO. You will also use these when you apply for other positions both within and outside of the company.

Remember that the goal in all of this is two-fold: **One is to raise awareness with your supervisor and within the company of your successes** and **the second is to keep an ongoing record of your contributions over time.** As your brand manager, you will be able to shape and mold the message about who you are and where you are going based on these self reviews. It will also help you, in this world of ever-changing people, to review with new bosses where you have come from and where you are going.

I have been amazed in my own career how often my bosses have changed. It is difficult with each change to re-meld into a new stroke and reorient yourself to a new boss with new goals and new ideas. It is your responsibility to bring them forward, to help them succeed AND to make sure that you have adequately informed them of your past contributions. It is *your* responsibility; you are your own Brand Manager.

Career death is made up of mediocre successes. You may not believe this now, but you learn infinitely more from a huge failure than you ever do from a so-so success. Coming out of a significant failure causes you to re-think. It helps you orient yourself to doing it much better next time. You don't have to experience the big failure to accomplish the same motivation. Commit to making a difference. Once you convince yourself you can, you will.

It is as easy as that. Then, be sure to advertise that success.

Remember that as women we often downplay our successes. This is NOT THE TIME to downplay your success. Use power words in your write up. You didn't just 'contribute to the successful launch of,' you 'organized and led the successful launch of.' Be sure to be truthful, but also to elaborate on what part you played. Use active verbs. Use more than one verb to describe the accomplishment. Our nature makes us want to humbly deny our participation or minimize it. However, we are competing for positions and PAY with men who are not wired to 'humbly deny' their participation. Because of this, men often seem more qualified and successful in their initiatives than we do. Give yourself credit. This is the time to lay humbleness aside. Recognize your contribution. Write it down. Work to proliferate your message across the corporation/company.

Winning Strategies Advice in Action: "Takeaways"
"Bethany, you are refreshing and motivating. My favorite takeaways are: seek out feedback and then do something with it, always know your strengths and how to use them, network, network, network, and be the CEO of your own career. This is great stuff that will help me immensely. Thank you!"
D.G., Mumbai, India

Where to Tout Your Successes Online – so Others Can Find You!

With this revised edition of *Winning Strategies for Women*, I chose to include a helpful Social Networking Summary Table from my book, *Brand YOU: A Step-by-step Guide to Building Your Brand* (© 2011). I provide this summary as a resource for your review in case you currently do not use, or perhaps have never heard of, these professional social networking tools.

Chapters 6-9 of *Brand YOU* are devoted to defining in detail the purpose and use of these sites for maintaining your digital, professional 'appearance.' Here is an excerpt from Chapter 6 to explain the purpose of those chapters.

"Your goal is for it to be easy for people to find you. If someone had a fantastic job offer for you, wouldn't you want him to be able to find you?

Make yourself findable [and tout your successes!]. The next few chapters will walk you through free internet options to raise awareness of who you are and allow you to brand and market your capabilities. We will also cover paid options to increase awareness of you or your company.

Through this amplified exposure plan, you will increase others' ability to find you when they reach out to find you."

Social Networking Summary Table	Description
Facebook http://www.facebook.com/	**Facebook** helps you connect and share with the people in your life.
Plaxo http://www.plaxo.com/	**Plaxo.com** is the world's leading online address book, hosting over 50 million address book accounts.
LinkedIn http://www.linkedin.com/	Over 150 million professionals use **LinkedIn** to exchange information, ideas and opportunities. Control your professional identity online, stay informed about your contacts and industry, and find the people and knowledge you need to achieve your goals.
HootSuite https://hootsuite.com/	**HootSuite** allows you to have multiple contributors to your social profiles without sharing passwords. Assign messages for follow-up and track responses. From help desk to marketing, engage audiences at every level of your organization.
TweetDeck http://www.tweetdeck.com/	**TweetDeck** is your personal real-time browser, connecting you across Twitter, Facebook, MySpace, LinkedIn, Foursquare, Google Buzz, etc.

[continued on next page]

Social Networking Summary Table	Description
Twitter http://twitter.com/	**Twitter** is a real-time information network that connects you to the latest information about what you find interesting. Simply find the public streams you find most compelling and follow the conversations.
Xobni https://www.xobni.com/	**Xobni** offers a unique and intelligent way to view and search your contacts and email through Outlook so you can spend less time searching for important information in your inbox & the web.
Spokeo http://www.spokeo.com/	**Spokeo** is a new-age white pages, aggregating data from many online and offline sources (such as phone directories, social networks, photo albums, marketing surveys, mailing lists, government censuses, real estate listings).
Talent.me https://talent.me/	**Talent.me** is a professional networking app on Facebook. Talent.me works to help you leverage your friend network and make it work for your career advancement.
BranchOut http://apps.facebook.com/ branchout/about/home	**BranchOut** is the largest professional network on Facebook.

Winning Strategies **Advice in Action: LinkedIn Profile Update**

"Bethany,
I updated my LinkedIn profile just a bit with some of the suggestions that you had in *Brand YOU* and I have had 6 serious recruiter pursuits initiate. I am starting a 3 month sub-contract consulting on Monday while negotiating with at least 3 full time job opportunities. I am stunned by the impact; a week ago I would have said that results like that were unbelievable! "
Laurel.S. , Burlington, Vermont

Winning Strategies **Advice in Action: Networking**

"Bethany,
I cannot tell you how much I enjoyed this morning's breakfast. I received multiple emails this evening from some of our ladies saying how much they enjoyed the speech and that they took away quality tidbits for their day.   I even had an email from one lady that does not network or leave her office, stating she needs to turn over a new leaf if there are fun events like this one out there.
Thank you for everything."
Maria S., Dallas, Texas

Chapter 11 "Touting Your Success from the Mountaintops" Summary of Key Points:

- Keep a folder of your successes
- Regularly advertise your success
- Create a biography if you don't already have one
- Annually write up a summary of your year
- Use Social Networking tools to stay connected and share your successes in a professional manner

Chapter Twelve

12. Communication Keys to Success

Communication is such a vital role in your success that this last chapter will prove to finish off the necessary ingredients to your success. Many jobs are won and lost over communication. Messages have been well received or poorly received based on how they are communicated. Email has given abilities to easily spread a message across a very wide audience in sub-second response time. This area can provide immediate benefit if you make significant changes. If you concentrate on communication, you will stand out. Most people are so busy these days that they are hurrying their communication. They are 'throwing up' in email- giving WAY TOO MUCH information for anyone to absorb. They are not selecting the text or the layout in a way to ensure the communication achieves the necessary goals. This is where my marketing skills came in very handy. I applied a marketing skillset to communication, and it took me a long ways. I will explain it to you in this chapter.

Email Therapy

Email can be both a valuable tool and a very harsh weapon. It is like a knife, knives can be used to chop tomatoes or to kill a man. We could not chop tomatoes without them, so they are a valuable tool. That same tool can kill people, so they are a dangerous weapon. Email falls into the same category.

Key Point: Email Can be Both a Valuable Tool and a Harsh Weapon.

It is like a knife, it can be used to chop tomatoes or to kill a man. Learn to use it wisely.

Emails rules to follow for success:
- ✓ Never use email to avoid the chain of command
- ✓ Clearly state your expectations
  - o Is the email for information only? State FYI, no action required
  - o Do you require an answer to move forward? State, Advice requested,
    Please respond by _____ (date)
  - o Would you like an approval?
    - ▪ Do you need that approval in writing? State, please email approval
    - ▪ No approval needed in writing? State, if no response within 7 days, I will move this initiative/project/task forward
- ✓ Only send necessary emails
  - o If you were cc'd and you are replying, there is no need to 'Reply All'
  - o Treat every email like it costs you $1 for every person that you email or cc
- ✓ Clearly state your objectives (more on this)
- ✓ Do not respond to an email when you are angry. IF the matter is urgent, and will cause conflict, pick up the phone.
- ✓ Make sure the Topic Line references what the email is about.

Imagine defending each email in front of a lawyer or a court of law. Imagine that your boss read all of your emails. These filters can often keep you in a professional tone and keep the message positive and accomplishing its intention.

Information comes at us in more ways than we can possibly review and 'think' on. At one point in my career, I had global product responsibilities for four product lines. I was getting anywhere from 130-150 emails a day that I needed to respond to, and several junk emails on top of that. I am sure that each person that emailed me imagined that I would be able to promptly respond to their emails. Each layer that you go higher on the ladder, the pressure and number of responsibilities grows, as do the number of emails that they receive a day. Think of email like getting your mail out of your mailbox every day. You sort through them and read the ones that are easy to read or respond to.

It is important to respect others' time in your emails. I advise you take a minimalist approach. Only send the email if you feel that it is VERY important. Minimize the number of words that you use in the email. Use **BOLD and *italicized*** words in your emails. Use colors for drawing attention to certain lines. Use bullets (•) to bring out key points, and **ALWAYS state your intentions** and what you expect them to do with your email. If it is URGENT- state Priority 1 or Urgent in the message line. If it is really urgent, then leave them a voice mail as well. Do not assume that they are connected to email when you need an urgent message. They may be on a flight, out of the country, or just sitting in meetings.

Winning Strategies for Women

Sample 1 "BEFORE"

Topic: Interfaces

Susan,
I will talk with Mark about the possibility of setting up interfaces between Product A and 3rd party product B this quickly, BUT - I need to know what interfaces to set up!

Product A needs to receive X from Product B - are we prepared to perform that action and send the patient information?

Product B will send DMI into Product A containing pointers to scanned images. We have to test this. It should be simple but has yet to work on the first try for any client. Do you need this interface for the demonstration (I'm sure you do). Who will be entering scanned images on Product B?

How will medical records information come to Product A in this scenario? Will it be via Medical Records Inbound? Will that come from Product C or from Product B? Will this interface have to be set up for the demonstration? How will Product B and Product C be interfaced? Will Mark have to set that up or is it a hotkey like in Product A?

How will Product B be updated to include the correct provider information to allow the interface messages to post?

Please keep in mind that this is not simple. Assuming that all three of these Product A interfaces are needed, we are talking about having the (client name) interface team set up and test six or eight separate interface threads on their network. It will take many hours of time on the part of the (client name) interface team. Right now they have not coded the MR inbound interface in their engine because we did not expect it to be needed. I expect that this effort will have an impact on conversions because we are using the same resources.

Sally Smith, Project Lead

Sample 1 "REDONE"

Topic: Interfaces

Susan,

I have received your request to facilitate discussions on the interfacing between **Product A** and **Product B** for **(Client Name).**

I have a few clarification questions:

　　1. Are we prepared to perform the action to send Patient Information from Product B to Product A?

　　2. Do you need the interface up and working that contains the pointers to the scanned images for the demonstration you mentioned?

　　3. Who can enter the scanned images on Product B?

I have scheduled a call to discuss specifics and walk through the scenarios so that I understand all of the details (like how medical records information will come into the Product A to begin with).

Internal Call- **Tuesday March 16, 200X at 2:00 PM.**

Please let me know if this time works for you. If not, please propose another time we could discuss this.

I look forward to talking to you about further detail. I understand that this is an important topic since the team necessary to do this work is also responsible for the conversion.

Sally Smith
Project Lead

The problem with the original email is that it really doesn't advise the reader what the writer is looking for. Emails like this first one, which I will refer to as the 'before' email, do not convey the necessary message nor do they accomplish the task at hand.

They are hard to read, and are often skimmed, missing vital information that inhibits progress at work. It causes you to communicate multiple times, rather than accomplish the desired result with one communication or email.

The most important things **to avoid** in an email:

- **TOO many words**
- **Things that are offensive**
- **Things that are obvious** need to be omitted

"Please keep in mind that this is not easy". If this had to be said, it certainly could be said in a better way. I don't believe it had to be said at all. It is offensive. It infers that the reader is inferior in their knowledge of the topic. Suggesting inferiority of your co-workers doesn't lead to getting more work done. Suggesting inferiority to your supervisor or boss leads to getting even less done!

The most important things **to communicate** in an email are:

- **Who the necessary parties are, if there are others aside from the ones the email was directed to**
- **Any applicable questions to arriving at next steps**

You want the reader to **feel:**

- **That you are capable of solving the problem**

- **That you respect him/her**
- **That you are glad that they are seeking your advice/resolution/expertise**

You want the reader to **understand:**

- **The objective**
- **What you want to be accomplished**
- **What the next steps will be to accomplish the objective**
- **What the writer WANTS THE READER TO DO with this information**
    - **Read it**
    - **Respond to it**
    - **Approve it**
    - **Schedule a call**
    - **Write a report**
    - **Escalate it**
    - **Communicate it**
    - **Etc.**

Most emails that I receive break one or all of the above rules. Often, they contain too many words. Many contain things that are offensive. Many state the obvious. Many do not state the objective of the email or what the next steps should be. And ALMOST all of them fail to TELL THE READER what YOU WANT THEM TO DO.

The most important thing that you can do in an email is to tell the reader how you expect them to respond. I cannot tell you how many emails I read and think, "hmmmmm, I wonder what they want me to do with this." Do they want me to call the customer? Do they want me to call the Project Executive? Do they want me to escalate it to the

CEO? It would be pure speculation on my part since the writer gave me no indication as to what they expected me to do with the information.

Sample 2 BEFORE (actual example pulled from business)

My advise is to have a small group discussion to confirm the documentation has been sent and for you to ask your question on client visits - Bill should be on the call just in case he has questions. I would probably skip the call - I'm actually off that day, taking my daughter on a college visit - but if I really need to participate I would make the effort to join, I land at noon MT. I then think we should have a follow-up call the following week to discuss any questions we might have on the document provided by Bill, discuss next steps, discuss (X company) (did this meeting happen this week?), discuss (city) visit (Roy working on this?). So, that is my advice. Let me know what you think.

Brown

Sample 2   REDONE

Topic: (client name)

My Advice:

- **Have a small group discussion this week** to confirm the documentation that was sent.

  - Ask questions about client site visits.
  - Include Rod in case he has questions.
  - I am on vacation this day so will be unable to attend unless you absolutely need to have me there. (Taking my daughter on a college visit - landing at 12:00 noon Mountain Time).

- **Have a follow up call the following week.**

  - Discuss any questions that we might have on the documents provided by Bill.
  - Discuss Next Steps
  - Discuss (X) company. (Did the meeting on this happen this week?)
  - Discuss visit to (X City). Is Roy working on this?

Let me know what you think.

Brown

Important email factors:
- **Layout**

- **Concise use of words**
- **Clarity**

These are actual examples. I really don't think you need to see more examples than these listed above. I am sure that your Inbox at work has more emails as described than you possibly need to review.

I am suggesting that you ensure that YOUR emails STAND OUT. I suggest you make sure that your emails are clear and concise. I suggest you clearly communicate what you need from the reader, and what you expect. I advise that you always state NEXT STEPS. In building your brand, make sure that you achieve your objectives and STAND OUT above the rest.

Communicating with your CEO and Other Top Level Executives

We all make the same mistakes, it seems, when we are communicating with the CEO and other top level executives. We want to EXPLAIN our case. We want to jump into the details to describe all the specifics surrounding it. Somehow, I think, that we fear that without the details, he/she will think that we don't know our job. It is quite the contrary. They know that you can do your job, or else you wouldn't be in it. They need VERY LITTLE explanation from you. They really need a few specific pieces of data.

I have prepared a checklist that you could review prior to your meeting. If you can't answer these questions, then you are not prepared for the meeting.

CEO/Senior Leader Meeting Check List

Are You Ready to Answer Each of These Questions?   Yes/No

☐   What solution do you propose?

☐   What is the resource and effort to solve this?

☐   Do you have it handled/under control?

☐   Do you need executive assistance?

☐   What specifically do you want Him/Her to do?

Circle all that apply

- Decision?

- Resource assistance?

- Support?

- Contact the client?

- Contact internal staff?

- Note: It's the right thing to share bad news

  - If it's on fire

  - If someone is free-falling - step in

    before they hit the ground

    "foresight is no good in hindsight"

Executives do not need the details. They need to know if you believe that there is a solution to the problem. They need to understand if there are resource requirements. They need to know if it is under control or if out of your control. They need to know if you need their assistance.

Key Point: Review the CEO Checklist Before a Meeting with the CEO.

Remember, it is not time to educate the CEO. Summarize the answers in opportunity statements to help to identify the big questions.

If you go through this checklist, and share the information in this order, your meeting should be a success. Do not dip into the details. They do not need them. Don't try to educate an executive. He/she doesn't have the time to learn all the specifics, and doesn't need that kind of data. Summarize the answers in opportunity statements and help to identify the big questions: what resources, how many, how long. If you don't know these answers, then explain how you will get the answers to these questions.

These are the notes that women that I've mentored took down when we covered the 'Communicating with the CEO' topic:

- Try not to educate your executive audience
- Try not to alarm executive staff (unless it is absolutely necessary)
- Executives don't care HOW it is solved, they want to know RESOURCES and EFFORT
    - Explain the resource and effort required or
    - Explain that you don't have it and will get it
- See attached check list (attached above)

Every Write Up/Assignment is a Term Paper

I was surprised in college that if your assignment didn't look AMAZING, then there was no way you could get an A. No matter what course it was, you were judged on content AND appearance. We somehow forget ALL of this when we get stuck in the hustle and bustle of an office where we have limited time and way too much to do. Suddenly, our attention switches to VOLUME instead of concentrating on making it A+ work. We work on 'getting it done', rather than making it SO GOOD that it stands out and really does what it was intended to do.

Your write ups, emails, and notes will either STAND OUT or FALL FROM EXISTENCE. Your goal is to make them stand out. You want to build an A+ brand for yourself. You want YOUR work to be known FAR ABOVE the rest. EVERY paper that you do will be judged. It will be rated. They will form an opinion of you, of it, and of your future.

Key Point: Build an A+ Brand Through Documents that Stand Out.

Make sure your work stands out above all the rest.

Every PowerPoint that you put together should be the best one the company has ever seen. EVERYONE should want to use your notes, your papers, and your emails. You know what they say, plagiarism is the best form of flattery. You want the masses to plagiarize your work. It should become the standard by which all others are measured. Many women have told me that they do not have time for this. Actually, you will find over time that you don't have time NOT to do this. If the work isn't REALLY good, then you will find yourself doing the assignment over and over again. If you do an exceptional job, I guarantee that you will not have to do it again and again. It will also stand the test of time. It will be re-usable for a period of time.

This has proven to be the most valuable information that I could give you. These assignments that you do should become your works of art. You should be proud of them. They should float around the company and become standards for others to follow.

Assure that your assignments have the following:
- Neatness
- AMAZING content
- Color & graphics

With each assignment, try to ensure that you have created another AMAZING document that will move your company forward. Try it; you will be amazed at the results.

Believing in Something and Being Willing to Fight for It

The best was saved for last. This section will separate you from the others. It will allow you to stand out from the crowd. It is imperative to be willing to fight for what you think is right. That belief extends to being willing to leave your job if the company is doing something that you believe to be wrong. It also includes being willing to leave your job if the company is making a decision that you know is not the right decision for the company. You are being paid wages/salary. With that, you accept some responsibility for the company's success. The higher you go up the ladder, the more responsibility you must accept.

Key Point: Speak Up for What You Believe In.

You will not lose your job for speaking up. On the contrary, you will be recognized and promoted if you speak up the right way.

I rarely find this quality in the workforce. Most believe that they must be silent and accept the decisions made, even if they are adamantly against them. Many have told me that they will not 'speak up' and risk losing their job. If you truly would lose your job for speaking up, then you are better off in another company. Do you want to work for a

159

company that is either A. making decisions that are not right ethically, or B. making decisions that are not going to lead to the success of the company and could even lead to a spiral of failure? Or even worse, do you want to work for a company that doesn't listen to the input of its employees? I advise against it.

Acceptable Reactions to Wrong in Your Company

As shocked as you may be that this is even a topic, consider the issues of the last few years with the scandals at Enron and Worldcom. Magnify how hard you've had to work to get the position you have, and I recognize that it has left some women vulnerable to accepting the status quo in order to stay employed. The percentage of women raising their children alone with no child support increases the difficulties we sometimes feel and the pressures to keep our jobs. Aside from all of these issues facing us today, I am advising that you stand up for what you believe in, and try to overcome the fears of job loss. If you do it the right way, your job should always be secure.

Acceptable Reactions

1. Notification: Always follow the chain of command. The first step is notification of your feelings directly to your boss/supervisor. I advise that this be both verbal and written. Meet with them to discuss your feeling and accompany it with a write up. This write up should be in some other media other than email.

Don't expect that they know how you feel or your position on the subject. Notify them with respect and without anger. Explain your stance, and allow them time to think on it and get back to you with their feedback. Ask for a definitive date for feedback.

2. Escalation: If your supervisor gets back to you and advises that there is nothing he/she can do, your next step is escalation. Let them know that your convictions require that you escalate this issue. You may be surprised. On several occasions I have had my supervisors say, at this point, that they are fine with me escalating the issue. I've even had them say, "Let me know what happens."

Occasionally, they will say that they would like to run it up the ladder one more time before you escalate it. This usually indicates that they never talked to anyone about the issue when you raised it. Either way, give them time to escalate it themselves if they choose to.

3. Action: If no answer and no action occurs, you then take action. You have several options.
- a) Call a Meeting with Key Leaders to Discuss
- b) Notify the internal Ethics Officer
- c) Talk to Human Resources

Key Point: Follow the Correct Path for Reactions to Wrong in Your Company.

Follow the path of notification, escalation, and action. By reacting in this order, you will give the company the chance to do the right thing.

Always work diligently to raise the issue within the company. Attempt to get the company to listen and solve the issue. It is not a good idea to go outside of the company until it is a last resort.

Standing Up for Your Beliefs

Sometimes, it is not a matter of simply black and white, right or wrong. Sometimes, it is a matter of what you believe to be right for the company. I ran into this in my career. I mentioned taking over the product line that had been sunsetted. The Product Manager before me, his name was Tom. He was in charge of the product line when it was determined that it would be killed. I asked him what he thought of that decision, after I took over. He said that he was appalled. He believed it to be a wrong decision. He felt powerless and felt that he had no choice but to accept the decision. Senior leadership had spoken. He did not go to them and express his discontent.

His position was to lead the product line. He was responsible ultimately for the future of the product. When leadership makes a decision you disagree with, you are REQUIRED to ADVISE LEADERSHIP if you DISAGREE ADAMATLY about their decisions. If you are leading a product line or a department or a team, they PAY YOU to speak up. If you are in a leadership position, THEY ARE PAYING YOU TO LEAD.

If you truly believe in something, you should be willing to stand in the unemployment line for that belief. I call it 'eating beans' for what you believe in, since that is what I use to eat a lot of when I had little to no money. Do you know what message you send Leadership when you stand up for something? You tell them that you mean it. You are

162

telling them in louder cues than you could ever say by simply raising your voice. Not only are you telling them that it a very important topic, but you are positioning yourself as a leader in that company. You are telling them where your character and your loyalties are. You are a company 'gal'. You want the company to make good decisions that will benefit both them and you. You look out for the company and raise issues if necessary. You want to make sure that the company is there in 2 years, 4 years, and even 10 years out. In order for that to happen, they must make good decisions, and you want to ensure that good decisions are happening.

Key Point: Be Willing to Stand in the Unemployment Line for Your Beliefs.

To be established as a true leader in your organization, you will need to speak out when leadership is running down an incorrect path.

You will run into leaders that surround themselves with 'Yes' people and DO NOT want to hear bad news or disagreements from you. I have found over time that even these leaders will respect your opinions if you do the following:

✓ **Don't be a chicken little**. Do not alarm someone in Leadership UNLESS absolutely necessary. If you believe that the company will figure the problem out and solve it, and that the worse that could happen is a slight delay in the timeline, then don't go out of your way to alarm exec leadership over it. Choose your battles.

✓ **Minimize the number of times you escalate** ANYTHING. They shouldn't hear from you more than twice a year. Use your 'escalations' wisely.

✓ **Spread the love.** All visits to leadership cannot be speckled with bad news and escalations. If you want to be heard, you must spend time stopping in or visiting leadership when you have NOTHING NEGATIVE to report on. Congratulate them on a recent sales deal, or a recent positive event that happened at the company. Ask them about their family. Say nothing negative.

✓ **Be consistent.** If you took a stance a year ago against something, don't change your opinion from year to year. Work is a bit like politics. Pick your platform and stick to it.

I once had a heart-to-heart with our CEO when I was ready to exercise my exit plan. I gave him a heartfelt plea for a part of the market that we were not pursuing. I felt that my skill set was not being utilized to its fullest if we did not pursue this sector of the market. I explained that I needed to be in a company that was pursuing the market that I had expertise and passion in. I told him that I thought we could be amazing in this market space, that we had the expertise and the passionate souls to get us there- but had not invoked the strategy and resourced accordingly.

He respected my heartfelt plea. He agreed to resource a part of the company to go after that market sector. He agreed to allow me to build a team to rebuild our product line in that area. It was not what I expected him to say.

When you do this, you will get results that you don't expect. If you shoot from the heart, you will lead where others have fallen. You will stand out from the crowds. You will be promoted when others are downsized.

So, the only thing holding you back is YOU. Your fear over losing your job is holding you back. The fear you have of 'speaking your mind' is holding you back. Your inability to ask for a raise is keeping your pay lower than the average. The ability to accept the status quo is limiting your potential and your future.

How do I know this? Because I have seen it in my own life. I have been able to quadruple my salary in only a few years. It doesn't matter your standing. It doesn't matter where you've come from or where you are today. I have been able to negotiate for stock options that have added 6 figure numbers to my bottom line. I have been able to rise to positions that others have told me I would never attain. You can do the same. I challenge you to try.

I'll be anxiously awaiting news of your success.

Chapter 12 "Communication Keys to Success" Summary of Key Points:

- Email can be both a valuable tool and a harsh weapon
- Review the CEO Checklist before meetings with the CEO
- Build an A+ brand through documents that stand out
- Speak up for what you believe in
- Follow the correct path for reactions to wrong in your company
- Be willing to stand in the unemployment line for your beliefs

Other books available by Bethany Williams:

Brand YOU: A Step-by-step Guide to Building Your Brand

In *Brand YOU: A Step-by-Step Guide to Building Your Brand*, Williams takes the reader through the process of personal brand development.   Create a distinct personal brand and message that sells you or your business to a market wrought with stiff competition. Get a job when others aren't!

"Your online personality should reflect your strengths and your accomplishments," Williams says. "Once your digital resume, or 'online billboard' has their attention, doors begin to open." It's not just about your skills and experience, but how you position your strengths and individuality. Read *Brand YOU* to catapult your job success.

Find it on the web: www.BrandYOUnow.com

From Mother to Mentor and Father to Coach

In From Mother to Mentor and Father to coach, Williams has created a guidebook to assist you in mentoring your teenagers to adulthood.

This book is brimming with practical tips and insights that **show you exactly how to move from parent to mentor**. You will learn to inform, not instruct. You will move into a position of information broker and less of president and CEO. You will become librarian and traffic cop, directing and facilitating your teenager, ensuring safety and education. Your role as parent officially changes to mentor.

Find it on the web at: www.BethanyAWilliams.com

Bethany Williams

Connect to the author via her web page:

http://www.BethanyAWilliams.com

She'd love to hear from you!

www.ingramcontent.com/pod-product-compliance
Lightning Source LLC
Chambersburg PA
CBHW051516170526
45165CB00002B/494